RESTORING
THE DREAM

RESTORING
THE DREAM

The Bold New Plan by
House Republicans

EDITED BY STEPHEN MOORE

TIMES BOOKS

RANDOM HOUSE

Contents

Acknowledgments

Restoring the Dream is the sequel to our earlier book, *Contract with America*, which outlined our bold agenda for the first hundred days of the 104th Congress. In *Restoring the Dream* we lay out a longer-term House Republican strategy for achieving a balanced budget, a reenergized economy, a strengthened family, and a leaner government that works for all Americans. Speaker Newt Gingrich and Majority Leader Dick Armey came up with the idea for the book. It was their visionary leadership that made *Contract with America* an unprecedented success. And it has been their vision about the direction that America must now be led that informs this book.

But the dozens of specific policy proposals contained here originated with the creative ideas of the individual 231 House Republican members. Some ideas come from the House leadership, some from committee chairmen, but, as you will see, we are pleased to report that many were inspired by our class of seventy-three freshman Republicans. They are the driving force behind the kind of bold change in Washington that Americans have been demanding for so long.

We should acknowledge at the outset that not every one of the 231 House Republicans endorses all the ideas presented in this book. Ours is a party of divergent views on many issues—a big tent. We may disagree on some of the specifics, but we all generally agree on the direction in which we want to lead America. There is nearly unanimous support among House Republicans that our overriding goal must be to end federal deficit spending by transforming our federal government.

Without Budget Committee Chairman John Kasich's unwavering leadership in preparing a road map for a balanced budget by 2002, this book would not have been possible. The Kasich budget plan is quite simply the most ambitious agenda for change in Washington in a quarter century. This book details many of the far-reaching proposals in that remarkable plan— one that will save taxpayers more than $1 trillion over the next seven years. We also wish to thank the Republican members of the House Budget Committee, as well as the energetic staff, especially staff director Rick May, all of whom have worked long into the night in recent months to deliver our fiscal blueprint to the American people—both on time and under budget.

The staff at the Republican National Committee also played an instrumental role in the preparation of this book. Chuck Greener and Mary Kate Cary of the RNC's communications office were absolutely critical in making sure that tight deadlines were met and in pushing the book through to its timely completion. Every time a potential roadblock appeared, they deftly steered us around it to make sure that the book became a reality. Research assistance at the RNC was provided by Dan Casey, Suzy DeFrancis, Harold J. Levey, and James E. Carter. Jonathan Knisley handled the graphics. And we want to thank Michael and Anna Gencarelli, who graciously loaned us what was to have been their time with their mother, Lisa McCormack, director of the RNC publications department.

Several congressional staff members reviewed the manuscript and provided helpful comments and criticisms. The list is extensive, and includes Kerry Knott, Ed Gillespie, and Michelle Davis with Majority Leader Dick Armey; Leigh Ann Metzger and Arnie Christianson with Speaker Newt Gingrich; and Paula Nowakowski with the House Republican Conference.

We also want to extend our special thanks to the Institute for Policy Innovation in Lewisville, Texas, which provided much of the data and research material in this book and allowed us to reproduce several of its graphs. The Institute's timely reports on budget and economic issues over the past several years were invaluable resource documents. IPI's director, Tom Giovanetti, generously lent us research material. For those who want to do further reading on the federal budget crisis, we recommend the Institute's booklet, *Government: America's Number 1 Growth Industry.*

Special thanks also to the Cato Institute for providing Stephen Moore a leave of absence to work on this book. Many of Cato's studies were also sources of helpful information.

Research assistance for the book was provided by Benjamin Geiger, Saguee Saraf, Jeanne Hill, Dean Stansel, and Allison Moore. Lisa Kruska was also a constant source of information and assistance. Perhaps no one's life was more disrupted by this book than that of Audrey Mullen of Americans for Tax Reform. Audrey provided research guidance, but more important, she allowed her basement to be converted into a makeshift office so the book could get written. For weeks, her downstairs was a litter of books, research materials, and manuscripts. Thanks Audrey. You can have your house back now.

Finally, and most especially, we want to thank the American people who take the time to read this book, and to share with us your comments and criticisms. Thank you in advance for joining our crusade to balance the budget, take on the special-interest groups, and make our government what it is supposed to be: a government of, by, and for the people. Our government can only be as good as its people. We see real goodness and concern in the American public about our fiscal crisis in Washington. That is why we are so confident that real change is not just possible, but imminent.

Foreword by
House Majority Leader
Dick Armey

HOUSE REPUBLICANS responded to the historic election results of 1994 in a way that was unique for Washington, D.C. We did what we said we would do.

In the first hundred days of the new Republican majority (the first ninety-three days, actually) we kept the promises we made in our *Contract with America*. Among the promises kept were passing the balanced budget amendment and line-item veto, replacing our failed welfare system with more compassionate solutions that encourage work and marriage, applying all laws to Congress and cutting one in three committee staff, cutting our own congressional budget, and providing tax relief for families who today need a second earner not to support the family but just to support the government.

By keeping our promises we helped restore the bonds of faith between the American people and their elected representatives, which was the intention of our *Contract*. In fact, at the end of our first four months, more Americans approved of Congress than disapproved for the first time in many years.

But our job is far from over.

We believe that America now stands at a crossroads. From time to time in the history of our great Republic, one generation is prevailed upon to keep the flame alive, to move the American experiment in representative democracy forward and not let it stall. Our Founders forged a union of states on the then revolutionary notion that we are all created equal. Abraham Lincoln preserved that Union and made all Americans free. Franklin Roosevelt summoned Americans of his generation to their "rendezvous with destiny." More recently Ronald Reagan set in motion the end of communism, expanding freedom to millions across the globe.

Always we were called to freedom, and always we responded. Today's generation of Americans are called to choose between two paths. One well-worn path is that of a constantly growing federal government and ever-increasing debt on our citizenry, the path of deficit spending as far as the eye can see. It is perhaps the path of least resistance, since it offers business as usual (and therefore little debate or risk to politicians) in the short term. It offers little hope, however, that our children and grandchildren might hold the same brightly burning torch of hope and freedom passed to us by those previous generations.

The other path is a new direction, a change in course from the one we've been on for the past twenty-five years. This new path moves toward long-term fiscal responsibility with a balanced budget by the year 2002, bridging the millennial divide with a commitment to continued freedom and prosperity in the twenty-first century. It is a path that says we will no longer pile so much debt on future generations that they will be forced to devalue our currency, sending the dollar the way of the Mexican peso. It is a path that says we will resist the pressure of the special-interest groups in Washington, and put the public interest first.

When I say we stand at a crossroads, I am not being hyperbolic. If current trends continue, in little over a decade spending on just five items will consume all the revenue of the federal government: Social Security, Medicare, Medicaid, Federal Retirement, and interest on the National Debt.

Any spending on programs like defense, school lunches, education, research, welfare, or any other budget item would come through borrowing. If we do nothing today, Medicare will go bankrupt in just seven years, and Social Security will follow. Each baby born this year will pay roughly $180,000 in federal taxes over his or her lifetime just to pay the interest on the national debt.

Changing familiar patterns of behavior, no matter how destructive they might be, is never easy. I suspect that by the summer of 1995 every family will be aware of the debate taking place in our nation's capital. The demagoguery quotient will be high and the noise level coming from inside the Beltway (the circle of highway surrounding Washington, D.C.) will be so loud that few Americans will be able to ignore it as they go about their daily lives.

That is why this book is important. As we have already seen, those who would preserve the status quo will resort to magnificent distortions to further their causes. So, discouraging illegitimacy in the welfare bill became "punishing children," increasing federal school nutrition programs by 4.5 percent annually (rather than 5.2 percent) became "ending school lunch programs." And efforts to preserve the solvency of Medicare became "attacks on the elderly." An uninformed public is a haven for the demagogue. This book, *Restoring the Dream*, tells people how changes can be made in federal spending that would get us to a balanced budget by the year 2002 *without* "taking food from poor children" or "throwing elderly widows out into the snow."

This book tells you what you can expect. In September 1994 we told you what you could expect if you honored Republicans with the first Republican majority in forty years, and then we did what we said we would do. Now we tell you what a balanced budget might look like seven years from today and the impact that such a budget would have on our economy and future generations. A balanced budget means that instead of a 9 percent thirty-year mortgage, you could get a 7 percent thirty-year mortgage, and interest rates on your car loan would also be two full percentage points lower. Our economy would boom, our children would prosper, and the promise of America would be kept alive.

But some federal programs would not grow as fast as otherwise projected, some would be cut (in the real-world sense of the word), and some programs would actually be eliminated altogether. For years Americans have said they want our nation's budget balanced, and that they were frustrated because the federal government was too big and spent too much. House Republicans are willing to test that proposition and to tell

Americans how exactly we would implement the change they have been demanding.

The public has not seen this kind of honesty before. We seek a new partnership with the American people to remake the budget in a way that is more efficient and responsive to our needs, while saving the future of this nation. I am full of unbridled admiration for my colleagues in Congress for having the courage to offer Americans such a choice and for engaging in the most consequential public-policy debate since the advent of the New Deal some sixty years ago.

The policies outlined in this book will give you a clear sense of the direction in which we want to go, but we will engage all Americans in the debate over how we ultimately get there. Even among House Republicans, I expect lively debate over many of the proposals to restructure government contained in *Restoring the Dream*. In the end, however, we will make the tough choices necessary—working in partnership with the American people—to secure the blessings of liberty for our children and grandchildren.

Please read this book closely. Your nation's future rests partly on your shoulders.

RESTORING
THE DREAM

I

Promises Made, Promises Kept

WHEN WAS the last time politicians in Washington kept their promises to the voters? By passing nine of the ten items in our *Contract with America,* and by doing so within the first hundred days of the 104th Congress, we have done just that. We have kept faith with the American people.

In a festive ceremony in front of the U.S. Capitol on September 27, 1994, 367 Republican candidates for the U.S. House of Representatives signed the *Contract with America.* We made concrete commitments to the voters. We said that we would require Congress to live under the laws it applies to everyone else; that we would give the President a line-item veto; that we would loosen Washington's regulatory stranglehold on businesses and property owners; that we would deliver a tax cut for families and a capital gains tax cut to reenergize our economy; and we assured you that we would pass a genuine, tough crime bill. And we made many other promises as well.

We kept them all.

For six weeks, we campaigned tirelessly in favor of the *Contract* as the blueprint to change business-as-usual politics on Capitol Hill. Liberal Democrats and the Washington Establishment fervently campaigned against it. A spirited and healthy debate developed on the proper direction of public policy in Washington.

Then, on November 8, 1994, voters all over America ratified the *Contract* by electing a Republican majority to the House of Representatives for the first time in forty years. We came to Washington and immediately got down to business. In January we set a grueling legislative pace to meet our self-imposed deadline of enacting the *Contract* before Washington's cherry blossoms were in full bloom. And to the surprise—and at times the despair—of political pundits, we did what we said we would do.

We proudly announce that the *Contract* has been signed, sealed, and delivered.

We recognize, of course, that Americans want far more than the ten items contained in the *Contract with America*. We do, too. The *Contract* was never meant to correct in one hundred days all of the unreasonable regulations, unfunded mandates, and unaffordable spending programs imposed on America by arrogant and out-of-touch Democrats in Washington. Think of the *Contract with America* as our down payment on the wholesale changes that we envision in order to prepare the federal government for the twenty-first century. For years Capitol Hill has served as a playground for liberalism. No more. Now we intend to clean up the mess—and, yes, start paying the bills. Our mission is to totally transform the government in Washington—to make it more cost-effective, citizen responsive, and fiscally responsible.

In this book we will describe in detail our agenda for extending the *Contract* by restoring the American Dream. This agenda involves such long-overdue ideas as strengthening the American family; replacing the welfare state with a genuine opportunity society; fixing our failing schools; forging a new partnership with our cities; and building a competitive and prosperous economy second to none in today's modern global marketplace.

The centerpiece of our plan for restoring the American Dream is to once and for all balance the federal budget. Deficit spending is already slowing America down. Like a cancer, it is gradually sapping America of the economic vitality that propelled us to number one in the world in living standards and productivity. Our nearly $5 trillion national debt has brought us perilously close to the brink of fiscal and moral bankruptcy. We pledge to work with the American public to fix this national crisis. If we cannot deliver, then voters should throw *us* out.

In 1995 we pledge to do something that no Congress in twenty-five years has done: to pass into law a fiscal plan that balances the federal budget of the U.S. government. The days of $200 billion and $300 billion deficits for as far as the eye can see are over. For the sake of our children and grandchildren, we will—no, we *must*—regain control of our economic destiny by balancing the budget and restoring the American Dream. But first, let's take a look at what we accomplished in our first hundred days.

THE FIRST HUNDRED DAYS

Our *Contract with America* was a unique undertaking in the history of American politics: we signed an ironclad promise with the voters across the country to accomplish ten specific legislative goals in one hundred days. We said to the American voters: if we don't deliver on this *Contract*, fire us. The motivation behind the *Contract* was to restore the trust between the people and their elected officials in Washington. Virtually all of the agenda items in the *Contract* were popular legislative initiatives—such as the balanced budget amendment, line-item veto, legal reform, and term limits—that had been bottled up by the Democratic-controlled Congress for decades. In a sense, the protectors of the old order in Washington had imposed a gag rule on democracy. Why? Because all of the *Contract with America* items, although popular with the public, are threatening to the power structure in Washington.

Many commentators have remarked that it is a sign of a new openness in Washington that we were simply able to bring each of these measures to a vote. We believe that the *Contract* sends four important messages to the American public:

> *One*, politicians—even in Washington—can keep their word.

> *Two*, the forces of political gridlock in Washington can be defeated; real change in Washington is possible.

> *Three*, the days of tax-and-spend budget policies on Capitol Hill are over.

Four, the public interest can be promoted
in Washington over entrenched special
interests.

Political commentator David Broder recently described
the positive impact on our system of democratic governance of what we accomplished. "It is healthy for
our politics—and politicians of any affiliation—when
the public sees elected officials doing what they
promised," he wrote.

DAY ONE: CONGRESS REFORMS ITSELF

No one can deny that when we came to Washington
in January we hit the ground sprinting. Indeed, many
Americans became aware of the broad, sweeping political reforms that we had in mind for our government
on the very first day of the new Congress. More popular laws were passed in our first twenty-four hours
than were passed in the twenty-four months of a typical Congress in recent years. Here is a rundown of
what we accomplished on just the first day of the GOP
takeover of Congress:

**First: Make Congress live under the laws it
imposes on the rest of the country.**
[Approved: 429–0]

For years, Americans were appalled to learn that
Congress exempted itself from the laws and regula-

tions it imposes on workers, businesses, and families. Here is a sample of laws that Congress had exempted itself from in the past:

- Civil Rights Act of 1964

- Civil Rights Act of 1988

- Ethics in Government Act of 1978

- Age Discrimination Act

- Equal Employment Opportunity Act

- Freedom of Information Act

- Age Discrimination Act

- Social Security Act of 1933

The long-prevailing arrogance in Washington—that Congress is above the laws that it imposes on the rest of us—has now been forever banished from our Capitol.

Second: Select a major independent accounting firm to conduct a comprehensive audit of the House of Representatives for waste, fraud, and abuse. [Approved: 430–1]

For the past forty years of Democratic control of the House of Representatives there was never an audit of how Congress spends money on itself. For instance, the finances of the scandal-ridden House Bank and House Post Office had never been independently examined until 1992, when Republicans put the pressure on for an audit. How many other financial scandals have yet to be uncovered because of congressional secrecy? We aim to find out.

Third: Cut the number of House committees and cut committee staff by one-third.
[Approved: 416–12]

With a $2.8 billion budget, Congress is by far the most expensive legislature in the world. In 1994 there were some 35,000 workers on congressional payrolls. That staff was nine times larger than any other legislative body in the developed world. Congress had succeeded in making the former Soviet Parliament look lean, mean, and efficient. In 1994 some 20,000 of these workers were directly employed by House members on their personal or committee staff. This was up from 11,000 in 1970; 4,000 in 1950; and 1,100 in 1930. As these numbers demonstrate, if we want government to become lean and efficient, Congress itself is an ideal place to start cutting—and so we have.

Fourth: Limit the terms of the Speaker of the House and committee chairs.
[Approved: 355–74]

The days when power-hungry, entrenched, and out-of-touch committee chairman reigned over the affairs of Congress for decades at a time are over. We have imposed eight-year term limits on committee chairmen. This even applies to the Speaker of the House.

Fifth: Ban the practice of proxy voting on congressional committees. [Approved: 418–13]

We have returned Congress to the simple democratic rule of "one man, one vote." This will end the practice of "ghost voting" in House committees, where nonpresent members delegate their vote to another member.

Sixth: Require all committee hearings to be open to the public. [Approved: 431–0]

This provision is a centerpiece in our pledge to bring new openness to your Congress. The veil of secrecy has been lifted. The House of Representatives is supposed to be the peoples' house. What, after all, does Congress have to hide from the public?

Seventh: Require a three-fifths vote to pass an income-tax rate increase. [Approved: 279–152]

Americans have been hit with twelve tax hikes in the past twenty years; each one has succeeded in further expanding the size of government instead of reducing the debt. Americans are starting to feel that Congress is trying to draw blood from a stone. To demonstrate our commitment to ending the tax-and-spend cycle in Washington, we will now require a supermajority to raise income taxes. (This would have blocked much of Bill Clinton's record tax hike in 1993.) Several states, including Colorado and Oklahoma, have enacted such measures, thus stopping tax increases dead in their tracks.

This measure caused enormous howls of protests on the House floor from tax-and-spend Democrats. The debate brought to light a key philosophical difference between the two parties: the liberal Democrats want to reduce the deficit by continuing to raise taxes. It is our pledge to balance the budget without a penny of new taxes.

Eighth: Guarantee an honest accounting of our federal budget by ending baseline budgeting. [Approved: 421–6]

Every year Congress tells the public that it "cut" the budget, but somehow the spending and the debt just keep climbing. In 1995 President Clinton said he "cut" the budget, but spending was up some $60 billion. How can this be? The answer lies in the deceitful practice in Washington called "baseline budgeting." Under this fraudulent concept, a spending cut occurs whenever Congress spends less than what it wants to spend. A few years ago, when Lee Iacocca was told of this practice, he fumed: "If we tried this in private business, they'd lock us up."

These eight measures were designed to help restore Americans' faith in their government and to clean up

Congress. That was a lot to accomplish in one day. But we were just getting started.

THE *CONTRACT WITH AMERICA*

Our *Contract with America* contained ten separate items. We pledged to give each of these measures a full and open debate and a fair up or down vote on the House floor within one hundred days. Each bill was meant to remedy many of the major problems facing Americans today, such as high taxes, crime, over-regulation, and the failed welfare state. We succeeded in bringing all ten of the *Contract*'s bills to the floor for a vote and passed all but one. (Only term limits—which, as an amendment to the Constitution, requires a two-thirds vote of approval—failed.) At the time of this writing, many of these bills are now pending approval before the Senate. Although the Senate, by design, works at a slower pace, we are convinced that when all is said and done, virtually all of these bills will be sent to President Clinton for his signature. Given the bipartisan approval of so many of these measures, and their broad-based popular support among the voting public, we are hopeful that the President will sign them into law. Let's examine the fate of the ten proposals contained in the *Contract:*

The Fiscal Responsibility Act

- *Balanced Budget Constitutional Amendment*
  [Approved: 300–132]

We are convinced that the balanced budget amendment is a vital first step in getting Washington's fiscal house in order. Recent opinion polls reveal that about 75 percent of the American public agrees with us and supports the amendment. Balancing the budget is not a mere accounting exercise. It's a moral imperative. It's about our children, the next generation, their dreams and their aspirations.

For too long, deficits have been Congress's preferred method of buying federal spending on the cheap. Why? Because the price tag for today's spending programs will not be paid for by today's voters, but by our children—who are more or less politically powerless. Each child born in America today inherits a charge of $180,000 in lifetime taxes just to pay the interest on the federal debt. The balanced budget amendment would end this form of fiscal child abuse immediately.

On January 26, 1995, the balanced budget amendment passed the House of Representatives for the first time in history. All but two of the then 230 Republicans voted for it. And we are pleased to report that this was a truly bipartisan effort: 72 Democrats joined us in supplying the votes needed to secure the two-thirds majority.

In the Senate, however, the amendment was defeated by one vote. We share the voters' anger and frustration. (Six Democratic senators who in the past had all supported the amendment—Tom Daschle of South Dakota, Byron Dorgan of North Dakota, Dianne Feinstein of California, Wendell Ford of Kentucky, Ernest Hollings of South Carolina, and Jeff Bingaman of New Mexico—flip-flopped and voted "no.") We are especially incensed that the Democrats who blocked the measure succumbed to special-interest lobbying and then resorted to fraudulent arguments to justify their votes. Social Security is not imperiled by a balanced budget amendment. In fact, the single most important step we can take to preserve the integrity of the Social Security system when the baby-boom generation retires is to end the torrent of deficit spending. Tomorrow's workers can't pay for Social Security if all their tax dollars are swallowed up, paying interest on a growing $5 trillion national debt.

The amendment has been defeated for now, but don't get discouraged. Majority Leader Bob Dole has pledged that he will bring this up for another vote in the Senate. The momentum is with us. We believe it is possible that the amendment will pass before the next election. Incidentally, in the four months that have passed since the amendment's defeat in the Senate, Washington rang up another $60 billion in debt.

- *Line-Item Veto* [Approved: 294–134]

The line-item veto allows the President to identify wasteful and excessive spending in a budget bill and use his veto pen to strike out the offending provision, while signing the rest of the bill into law. As such, the line-item veto is an antidote to pork-barrel spending. It allows the President to cut out the midnight basketball programs, the Lawrence Welk Museums, the Belgian endive subsidies, shark research, and the hundreds of millions of dollars of other frivolous projects that pollute our budget each year. The line-item veto will not balance the budget. But budget experts think that it could save $5 billion to $10 billion a year in wasteful spending.

Does this measure give too much power to the President?

No, and a quick history lesson proves why. The line-item veto is only a partial restoration of the budgetary powers of the President, which were stripped from the executive branch by the 1974 Budget Act. That act took away the President's right to impound funds. Impoundment was an extremely powerful White House authority that was exercised often for nearly two hundred years. Presidents Roosevelt, Kennedy, Johnson, and Nixon used the impoundment power routinely— and in some years used it to cut federal appropriations by more than 5 percent.

In 1974 Congress stripped the President of his impoundment powers and instead gave him two weak substitutes: the deferral and rescission authorities. Rescissions require Congress to pass with a "yes" vote a presidential request not to spend money. Most rescissions are simply ignored by Congress and never even voted upon. Thus, through congressional inaction, they are routinely squashed. Twenty-six billion dollars of Ronald Reagan's rescissions died a quiet death this way.

The line-item veto is a normal executive power on the state level. Forty-three governors have this budget-cutting tool. A recent survey of governors found that 92 percent believe that "a line-item veto for the President would help restrain federal spending." As Ronald Reagan once said, "When I was governor of

California, the governor had the line-item veto, and so you could veto parts of the spending in a bill. The President can't do that. I think, frankly—of course, I'm prejudiced—government would be far better off if the President had the right of line-item veto."

For many years pro-spending Democrats would not even allow an honest vote on the line-item veto. But on February 6, 1995, we banded together with conservative Democrats to approve the measure. We think this proves our good-faith determination to cut spending. How ironic that the first President to cut out wasteful spending with the new veto scissors will be Democrat Bill Clinton. We can only hope the President uses this new budget reduction tool early—and often.

The Taking Back Our Streets Act

In today's America, millions of our citizens feel unsafe walking after dark—and sometimes before dark—down their own street. We are a nation terrorized by crime and senseless acts of violence. In the time it takes you to read this page another two robberies and another three aggravated assaults will have occurred somewhere in America. In about the time it takes you to read this chapter another three women will have been raped. For far too long we have allowed a predator class among us to reign undeterred. For far too long we have failed to take tough measures that would empower us to take back our streets from the drug dealers, gangs, and sexual predators in our midst.

In 1994 the Democratic-controlled Congress passed a pork-laden crime bill. Indeed, in many respects it made a mockery of the war against crime. Republican efforts to improve the law enforcement provisions of the bill were blocked. Instead, the bill was crammed with some $8 billion of new social spending masquerading as crime prevention, programs like arts and crafts and modern dance classes, Olympic-sized swimming pools, and midnight basketball leagues.

The public knows that more social-welfare spending is not the answer to the scourge of crime. If it were, our inner cities would have the safest streets in the world. We've spent $2.5 trillion on social programs in cities over the past thirty years—and crime is worse than it was before this massive infusion of funds.

We promised in the *Contract* to fix Clinton's crime bill, and we did. Our approach is different. We think that if America is going to win the war on crime, it will be won in the neighborhoods where police and prosecutors band together with homeowners and residents to take back our streets one block at a time. The solution to this crisis surely will not be handed down from bureaucrats in Washington. But we do think that tough-on-crime measures that make punishment swift and severe will assist local law-enforcement efforts. Thus, we passed the following bills, which, taken together, constitute the toughest crime package approved by the House of Representatives in decades:

- *Mandatory Victim Restitution* [**Approved: 431–0**]

No longer will victims be the forgotten casualties of violent crime. Our bill requires criminals to pay full restitution for damages caused as a result of federal crimes.

- *Additional Spending for Prison Construction*
  [Approved: 265–156]

This bill authorizes $10.5 billion of funding for new state prison construction, up from $8 billion in Clinton's bill. A condition of these funds is that states keep their violent criminals behind bars. To receive funds, states must now comply with truth-in-sentencing guidelines, which require convicted felons to serve at least 85 percent of their sentence, before being released from prison. Studies show that 40 percent of crimes are now committed by convicts released early from prison.

- *Law Enforcement Block Grants* **[Approved: 238–192]**

This bill eliminates the social spending in the Democrats' bill and allows states and localities to use these funds for genuine law-enforcement programs, such as putting more cops on the street or buying new crime-fighting equipment. This approach saves $1.4 billion over five years.

- *Good Faith Exemptions to the Exclusionary Rule*
  [Approved: 289–142]

This bill allows prosecutors to use evidence in court gathered by law-enforcement officers acting without a warrant, but in good faith and not unreasonably. This will help prevent violent criminals from avoiding conviction based on minor technicalities.

- *Limitations on Death Penalty Appeals for Capital Crimes* [Approved: 297–132]

This bill places a one-year limitation on the filing of death penalty appeals. This act will facilitate the swift execution of convicted cold-blooded murderers, such as those responsible for the bombing of the federal building in Oklahoma City.

- *Deportation of Criminal Aliens* [Approved: 380–20]

States today spend hundreds of millions of dollars imprisoning illegal aliens convicted of violent crimes. This bill facilitates the deportation of criminal aliens who are in the United States without a green card.

The Personal Responsibility Act
[Approved: 234–199]

Is there anyone left in America who still defends the current welfare system? Bill Clinton has repeatedly pledged to "end welfare as we know it." Opinion polls reveal that Americans view the modern welfare state as an expensive failure. And it seems every day we are confronted with new statistics that underscore this failure: rising illegitimacy, expanding welfare rolls, increasing gang violence, and ever-escalating crime levels in our inner cities.

Welfare cheats the poor and perpetuates poverty. A child of a parent on welfare today is three times more likely than the average citizen to be on welfare when he or she becomes an adult. Since the welfare state was conceived in the 1960s, two generations of Americans have been sucked into the system and permanently trapped in the hopelessness and despair of welfare dependency. Our *Contract with America* was the first major step toward uprooting this corrupting system before it ruins the lives of yet another generation of Americans.

The Personal Responsibility Act was designed to be our first step in truly ending welfare as we know it. Highlights of the bill included:

• Giving states maximum flexibility in developing their own welfare programs. We think ultimately the solution to the welfare crisis will come from experimentation in states, not top-down control from Washington.

• Requiring work in a public or private sector job as a condition of welfare after two years on Aid for Families with Dependent Children (AFDC). The Act limits AFDC benefits to five years.

• Prohibiting AFDC and public housing to unmarried mothers under the age of eighteen. A mother on AFDC will no longer receive an additional cash benefit for having another child out-of-wedlock. We are through subsidizing teenage illegitimacy.

- Returning AFDC, child nutrition, and child-care programs to the states. Federal funding will be capped and provided in the form of a block grant. This will finally end the open-ended entitlement nature of welfare—the feature that has so escalated federal taxpayers' costs.

- Making most noncitizens ineligible for welfare programs.

- Ending Supplemental Security Income payments to drug addicts and alcoholics.

- Enforcing child support so that deadbeat parents can no longer escape the responsibility of paying for the rearing of their children.

The Family Reinforcement Act

We believe that for too long government policies in Washington have been tragically undermining the American family. The family is the core of our society. It is the mechanism through which we transmit values, knowledge, and discipline. Government can never serve the role of surrogate parent. But increasingly, through a vast network of ill-conceived economic and social policies, Washington tries to do just that. For example, we have failed to establish tough penalties against child pornographers and sexual predators who molest children. The distribution of condoms to twelve-year-olds in public schools attacks traditional values, such as abstinence, that we as parents try to instill in our children at home. Other government policies make it prohibitively expensive for young families to care for elderly parents who must then be placed in nursing homes.

Similarly, there are hundreds of thousands of couples in America who wish to adopt and give a child the love and nurturing it needs. At the same time we have thousands upon thousands of abandoned and abused children trapped in institutions who long for the security of a safe home. Government policies and federal social workers often discourage rather than encourage adoption. We approved two measures to strengthen families and protect children:

- *Family Privacy Protection Act* [**Approved: 418–7**]

This Act requires parental consent requiring children to participate in federally funded programs.

- *Sexual Crimes Against Children Act*
  [**Approved: 417–0**]

This Act imposes tough and swift criminal sentences against child molesters and child pornographers.

The American Dream Restoration Act
[Approved: 246–188]

Few would disagree with the statement that the most vital investment in our nation's future is our children. But children are an expensive investment.

One reason for the high cost of raising kids these days is that taxes on families have been rising steadily over time. The Heritage Foundation notes that the typical middle-income family of four paid just 2 percent of its income in taxes in 1948; today, that same family would pay about 24 percent of its income to the federal government. Over this same period the personal exemption's value has declined from 42 percent of family income to 11 percent.

Taxes on families are higher because the tax exemption for raising children has been eroded by inflation over the past thirty years. The value of the dependent exemption is now $2,400. It would have to be roughly $8,000 if it was worth what it was some forty years ago.

Another counterproductive federal tax policy is that we financially discourage families from saving for their future. We want to restore the concept of the Individual Retirement Account (IRA) which allows families to put $2,000 a year into a tax-free savings account. Unlike conventional IRAs, the funds placed in these savings accounts would not be tax free at the time of deposit, but rather at the time of withdrawal. We would allow families to withdraw funds from the IRA for the purchase of a new home, or for the education of their children, or for medical costs. These are all vital investments that pay dividends to all of society in the long run.

Finally, we think it is absolutely absurd that our tax code penalizes marriage through something called "the marriage penalty." Two single, middle-income people who live together and earn $40,000 each would pay about $1,200 more in taxes if they were to get married. Where is the tax fairness in that?

The American Dream Restoration Act strengthens families by:

- Establishing a $500-per-child tax credit for every family earning up to $200,000.

- Creating an American Dream Savings Account. This establishes a $2,000 tax-free IRA for all families and allows the funds to be withdrawn without penalty for retirement, the purchase of a first home, for college or to cover training expenses, and for unexpected medical expenses.

- Repealing the marriage penalty in the tax code once and for all.

- Providing adoption assistance through a one-time $5,000 tax credit for low- and middle-income parents to help cover the expenses associated with adopting a child.

- Offering a $500 tax credit for families who choose to care for an elderly parent or grandparent in their home.

The tax cuts in the American Dream Restoration Act have been criticized by some as being "unaffordable" in an era of large deficits. They actually represent only 2 percent of the revenue the federal government is already scheduled to collect over the next five years.

But we would emphasize that our tax cuts will not raise the deficit by a single dime. In fact, the bill helps cut the deficit. How? Every dollar of tax relief in this Act is paid for by an even larger reduction in federal spending. We make a straightforward argument for the $500 child credit: if you as a parent go out to work and earn the money, should you spend the $500 or should a bureaucrat? We choose the parents; our critics choose the bureaucrat.

The National Security Restoration Act
[Approved: 241–181]

Who can forget the malaise of the late 1970s when a liberal Congress so drastically cut our national defense budget that all we had left was a hollow military? Jimmy Carter's strategy seemed to be "peace through weakness." We were unprepared to deal with even third-rate military thugs, such as Iran's Ayatollah Ruholla Khomeini.

Never again. Ronald Reagan rebuilt our military arsenal and laid the groundwork for the collapse of the Soviet empire and a freer, safer world. But now that we have won the Cold War, we must not disarm ourselves as we have shortsightedly done in the past. The world is still a dangerous place.

We are concerned that, under President Clinton, American troops have been spread too thinly across the globe. This poses a real threat to our security. In just the past year Clinton's adventurism sent American troops to Haiti, Macedonia, Rwanda, and the Persian Gulf. Last year, America was involved in thirteen separate peacekeeping operations around the world—many of these under the auspices of the United Nations and with highly dubious U.S. national-security interests at stake. Yet, increasingly, military experts worry that we don't have an adequate support structure in place to fully protect American soldiers should flare-ups occur. Defense spending is now less than 4 percent of the Gross National Product—its lowest level as a share of national output since Pearl Harbor.

Provisions in our *Contract with America* take the following steps to strengthen American national security:

- We make it much harder to put U.S. troops under UN or foreign command and cut funding for international "peacekeeping." American troops should always and only be fighting alongside the American flag.

- We prevent Congress and the administration from robbing the defense budget of dollars in order to continually fund more domestic social programs. Wherever we can save money in the defense budget, the savings should be used to reduce the deficit and the tax burden on families.

- We create a blue-ribbon panel of military experts to conduct a comprehensive review of our national defense spending, readiness, and modernization to ensure that we are getting full value for our defense dollars while protecting our vital national-security interests.

The Senior Citizens Fairness Act
[Approved: 424–5]

America's tax code is increasingly hostile to working senior citizens. Because of all the special taxes that we impose on the elderly—such as taxes on Social Security benefits and the earnings test on working Americans between sixty-five and sixty-nine—we seem intent on driving them out of the work force and into full retirement—often against their will. President Clinton's tax hike on seniors in 1993 made a bad situation worse. Though the White House continues to allege that it raised taxes only on "the wealthy," the truth is that senior citizens with incomes as low as $34,000 got hit with a Social Security benefit tax hike. Now 85 percent of these workers' Social Security benefits are taxed. We doubt that many seniors making $40,000 or $50,000 a year consider themselves in the category of "the undeserving rich."

The most unfair tax on the elderly is the Social Security earnings test provision. The earnings test says to working seniors: for every dollar you earn over $11,160, we're going to take 33 cents away from you. The policy is anti-work, anti-senior citizen, and anti-tax fairness. The earnings test seems to send a simple message to even moderate income seniors: stop working.

Our Senior Citizens Fairness Act corrects these gross inequities by:

• Repealing Bill Clinton's Social Security benefits tax.

• Raising the Social Security earnings test income threshold from $11,160 to $15,000 in 1996, and eventually to $30,000 by the year 2000.

• Establishing tax incentives to allow Americans to purchase long-term care insurance to protect them from the financial ruin that often accompanies large medical expenses as we grow older.

So our message to seniors is quite different from that of President Clinton and past Congresses: we want you to lead the fullest and most productive lives possible in your golden years. We won't punish you for working or investing in order to supplement your Social Security check.

The Job Creation and Wage Enhancement Act [Approved: 277–148]

The Founding Fathers viewed the protection of private property, along with life and liberty, as the primary purpose of government. The Fifth Amendment to the Constitution explicitly states: "No person shall . . . be deprived of life, liberty, or property, without due process of law; nor shall private property be taken for public use, without just compensation." Yet thanks to the insidious proliferation of regulations, government takes property today without "just compensation" all the time. Often these "regulatory takings" are justified in the name of environmental protection. For example, by declaring private property a wetlands or a sanctuary for an endangered species, government can prohibit any development on the land, thus depriving it of most of its value. From the point of view of the landowner, such regulation has much the same effect as if the government had actually seized the property—except in that case the state would be forced to pay "just compensation."

To prevent this continued erosion of Americans' property rights, our *Contract* bill requires the federal government to fully compensate landowners for any government agency action that limits property usage and diminishes its value by 20 percent or more. Compensation is not required when the federal action limits actions on one's property that prevent a hazard to public health or safety. This Act would still permit environmental and land-use regulation, but would simply require that the cost be borne by the society as a whole, rather than the private owner.

The Common Sense Legal Reform Acts

Today America has the majority of the world's lawyers (most of whom live in Washington, D.C., of course), who file more than 18 million lawsuits a year. In 1991 the Vice President's Council on Competitiveness reported that frivolous lawsuits and outlandish damage awards cost the economy up to $300 billion per year in indirect expenses. These expenses add to the costs of every good and service we buy. They are the equivalent of a $2,800 tax on every household in America.

Excessive litigation imposes other indirect negative effects on the economy. Here are just a few examples: diversion of business time and effort to fighting off nuisance lawsuits; overloaded court dockets and thus expensive delays; unnecessary defensive medicine to prevent malpractice suits; and a reluctance to bring new products to market for fear of product liability lawsuits.

We want to insure that every American has full access to our legal system, but at the same time we want to discourage extraneous expenses and frivolous lawsuits that drive up the cost of the system for everyone. Predictably, the powerful and well-financed trial lawyer lobby has been fighting us every inch of the way. They charge that the victims of these measures are the poor, who will be deterred from bringing legitimate suits. The truth is these reforms, especially the "loser pays" rule, actually allow for swifter resolution of strong cases. No, the victims are not the poor. The only "victims" are the wealthy trial lawyers who have been feeding off of an unfair and inefficient legal system for far too long. Here then are the common-sense ideas we passed:

- *Attorney Accountability Act* [**Approved: 232–198**]

The act discourages frivolous lawsuits by instituting a modified "loser pays" system, which subjects both sides to the costs of their opponent's legal fees if either side rejected a settlement and went on to win something less at trial. The bill also requires judges to impose sanctions on attorneys for making frivolous arguments and ends abuses of "rent-an-expert witness" practices that have proliferated in this last decade.

Many of these "experts" are simply peddling junk science. We would render inadmissible any expert testimony not based on "scientifically valid reasoning."

- *Common Sense Product Liability Reform Act*
  [Approved: 265–161]

This Act reforms the product liability laws and caps punitive damages at $250,000 or three times the actual harm, whichever is greater. It also creates sanctions against parties that bring frivolous liability suits.

- *Securities Litigation Reform Act*
  [Approved: 325–99]

This Act limits shareholder lawsuits against companies whose stocks experience abnormal price volatility. These so-called strike lawsuits are often brought as a result of speculative investments that lose money for the shareholders. In the last two years alone, firms have had to pay out $500 million in shareholder suit settlements. About 40 percent of these securities fraud charges are brought against start-up high-technology firms—whose stocks tend to be risky and volatile to begin with. Ed McCracken, cochairman of the American Entrepreneurs for Economic Growth, a network of small business CEOs, protests that these shareholder lawsuits often wind up being little more than "moneymaking vehicles for plaintiffs' lawyers." The evidence supports that charge. The average plaintiff attorney fee in successful suits exceeds $2 million. In one recent record-breaking judgment, investors received $4 million and attorneys $8 million.

In one recent case, Exabyte, a Boulder, Colorado, firm that manufactures computer tape drives, saw its stock sink from $24 to $15 a share after a quarter of poor earnings. Within three weeks the firm was slapped with eight lawsuits, all filed by the same law firm, all of which were eventually dismissed by the courts. Yet for a firm like Exabyte the cost of winning was staggeringly expensive. The American Entrepeneurs for Economic Growth reports that the average firm spends $700,000 in legal fees and 1,000 hours of management time fending off a frivolous lawsuit. In entrepreneurial industries this has become a standard cost of doing business, thus reducing firm profitability, investor return, and American competitiveness. We agree with Democrat Rep. Billy Tauzin of Louisiana who insists that in too many of these strike suits the real "fraud" is "being perpetrated by a small number of predatory attorneys and plaintiffs. The defendants are the victims."

The Citizen Legislature Act [Failed: 227–204 (288 needed for two-thirds)]

The long experiment in professional politicians and professional government is over, and it failed. The overwhelming majority of the American people recognize this. They have voted for term limits on their state and local elected officials all over the country. Twenty-three states have voted to impose term limits on Congress.

Term limits will attract a different caliber of person to office—the citizen legislator. We will have fewer lawyers representing us in Washington, and more small-businessmen and small-businesswomen, community leaders, teachers, and doctors. We will have elected leaders who have signed the front side of a check, not just the back. All of this will be healthy for democracy.

For more than ten years, the Democratic leadership in Congress prohibited even a *vote* on term limits in the House of Representatives. We promised to end the conspiracy of silence on this issue and fulfilled our *Contract* promise to have an up or down vote on this vital issue.

Unfortunately, the constitutional amendment that we brought to the House floor was defeated. Not surprisingly, some politicians in Washington are not enthralled with the idea of imposing term limits on themselves. Still, our vote made it clear which party is the enemy of term limits, and which is mostly in favor of this reform. Eighty-two percent of Republicans voted for term limits. Less than 20 percent of Democrats voted for them.

The term limit vote in March 1995 was only a temporary setback. Term limit advocates have made it clear that they won't be denied. As such, we have pledged that the first bill that we bring to the floor in January 1997 will be term limits.

ONE HUNDRED DAYS—AND BEYOND

As you can imagine, passing all of these measures in one hundred days (actually, in ninety-three days to be exact) was an exhausting and exhilarating endeavor.

Many commentators are now conceding that what we have accomplished in the first hundred days is perhaps the most far-reaching slate of reforms to pass Congress in fifty years. For example, *USA Today* compared the *Contract*'s completion to "the vast social and political changes heralded by Franklin Roosevelt's New Deal and Lyndon Johnson's Great Society. Like the 1930s and 1960s, the Nineties hold the promise of another generational swing—to smaller government, less regulation, and toward lower spending and regulation." Even *The Washington Post* tipped its hat to us the day after the *Contract* was completed. The *Post*'s assessment was that by delivering on the *Contract*, "the House Republicans have reinvigorated what had become a tired arm of national government and set a standard of boldness in the use of political power that will likely be invoked in judging new administrations and Congresses for years to come."

Probably no American agrees with every single measure in our *Contract with America*. But few Americans would disagree that most of these laws were long overdue. In fact, as one scans the items in the *Contract*, it seems remarkable that it took so many years for many of the most popular and noncontroversial measures to be passed.

What are we to make of the critics in Washington who remain so arrogantly contemptuous of the *Contract with America*? They snort that the new laws we have passed are misguided and trivial—that they will have no impact on people's lives. (Remember: these are many of the same people who gleefully predicted in December 1994 that we would never be able to pass so many far-reaching measures in just one hundred days.) When we passed these items one by one they jeered our progress. And when we failed to pass term limits, they jubilantly proclaimed that the GOP was in disarray and that the *Contract* was unraveling.

These were the voices of the protectors of the old order. Their concern is to protect and preserve the bureaucratic empire they have spent their careers in Washington erecting. They are the opponents of change, the agents of gridlock. They are elitists who oppose giving Americans the government they want and deserve. They have misidentified the winners and losers. The losers are the special-interest groups in Washington; the winners are the working men and women across America who have been demanding these changes for years.

For those in Washington who insist that our agenda was too extreme and too right-wing, we think there are at least 2,971 reasons to think that they are wrong. The ten *Contract* items included thirty-one separate roll-call votes. Democrats, collectively, voted "yea" a total of 2,971 times. Forty-seven percent of the time the Democrats voted with us in approving the *Contract*. The *Contract* was "extremist" only if half the Democrats in Congress are, too.

But our big-spending critics in Washington still don't get it. They don't understand that working Americans *do* want a balanced budget amendment, and tough anti-crime measures, and a line-item veto, and tax cuts for their families, and a capital gains reduction to create jobs. They *do* favor legal reforms, a strong national defense, and term limits. And we are convinced that

Americans of all income groups are hugely relieved that the tax-and-spend days on Capitol Hill are over.

So we have signed, sealed, and delivered the *Contract with America*. But we are far from done. We have always viewed the ten items in the *Contract* as only the first critical steps in our mission to restore the American Dream and transform government in Washington. We want to make the federal government work again for its citizens. The *Contract* was an exciting and productive first round of political and economic reforms.

Now we are prepared to make another pledge to the American people: You ain't seen nothing yet.

2

Restoring The American Dream

THE *CONTRACT WITH AMERICA* was the first step of our journey to restore the American Dream for all our citizens—whether they live in Los Angeles or Harlem. The American Dream is about a basic optimism that the future will be better than the past, that anyone in America, no matter what their income level, or where they were born, or what their skin color is, can succeed through perseverance, education, hard work, thrift, and taking risks. This is another way of saying that America is still a land of opportunity.

Or is it? Sadly, Americans seem to be losing faith in the Dream. A recent public opinion poll revealed that increasing numbers of our citizens view the American Dream as slipping out of their grasp. For example, a 1994 Luntz poll showed that Americans, by a two-to-one margin (61 percent to 31 percent), fear the "next generation's standard of living" will be worse than their own. A growing percentage of younger Americans now say they would be satisfied to achieve a living standard comparable to what their parents have attained.

These findings indicate a deeply rooted economic anxiety among American citizens. Many Americans say they feel as if they are on an economic treadmill—running faster and faster, not to get ahead, but just to stay in place. Some experts interpret these anxieties as a sign that a malaise has taken root in the United States—a crisis of the American spirit. Those who think this generally believe that America is an empire in gradual economic descent. Historian Paul Kennedy is one of the leading proponents of this declinist theory. He writes in his best-selling book *Preparing for the Twenty-First Century* that he foresees an America undergoing "slow, steady, relative decline—in comparative living standards, educational levels, technical skills, social provisions, industrial leadership, and, ultimately national power." That's a dreary portrait of America in the next century—and it is shared by many of our doom-and-gloom intellectuals.

We reject this prognosis. Most of what is wrong with America today is a result of years of bureaucratic empire-building in Washington and a long-standing liberal mindset that whatever is wrong, government will fix it. Liberalism's fixes—welfare, urban handouts, public housing, the Department of Education—are now visible and widely acknowledged failures. The resounding rejection of Clinton's attempted government takeover of the U.S. health-care industry was perhaps the turning point. Americans rose up in huge numbers and said: enough is enough; we've had enough of your false promises and expensive failed solutions.

Unfortunately, Washington doesn't cope well with failure. In real America if something isn't working, we stop doing it and try a new approach. In Washington if something isn't working, we conclude just the opposite: the program needs more money. During the debate on our welfare reforms in *Contract with America* we heard some of our critics suggest that the $5 trillion welfare state has spent too little to help the under-class, rather than acknowledging that the system just isn't working. Liberal faith in government is seemingly bottomless: given enough money, there is no social, economic, or moral crisis that Washington can't solve. For too long the prevailing ethic in Congress has been this simple—or rather, this simple-minded.

To fully restore the American Dream and to make government work for its citizens again, we need to lay to rest the fiscally ruinous mindset in Washington of limitless taxpayer resources. We need to scour through every nook and cranny of the government fortress and start terminating many of the floundering federal agencies, offices, and programs which have been spawned over the past thirty years by that bankrupt dogma.

When government begins to provide true value for our tax dollars, and reforms its institutions so they deliver a quality, cost-effective product, government in Washington will once again be a partner—instead of an obstacle—to the American Dream.

A CENTURY OF PROGRESS AND PROSPERITY

The twentieth century has been the American century. The United States has experienced a spectacular rate of sustained economic progress unparalleled in all of human history. In fact, the advances have been so rapid that many Americans cannot fully appreciate how far this nation has progressed in a very short time.

According to a recent Institute for Policy Innovation report, throughout most of this century the American economy has accelerated at a rate of between 3 and 4 percent per year. Since 1900 incomes of American families have doubled roughly every twenty-five years. In other words, throughout this century every generation of Americans has succeeded in achieving a living standard that is almost twice that of its predecessor. The average American today is six times richer—in real inflation-adjusted dollars—than the average American living in 1900.

This constant improvement in our economic and material condition is the essence of the American Dream. Continuous progress is America's economic manifest destiny. This income growth is attributable largely to the phenomenal productivity of the American worker. Manufacturing output per man-hour has more than quadrupled since 1930. In other words, what took a worker an hour to produce sixty years ago is now produced by an American worker in fifteen minutes or less. That success almost pales compared to the gains made by the American farmer. Today the American farmer is ten times more productive and efficient than his counterpart in 1900.

The good news is that the American worker is still Number One. In 1992 the average American manufacturing worker produced 20 percent more than the average Japanese and German worker and at least 25 percent more than the typical British worker. The bad news is that our lead is slipping and our competitors are catching up. If we stay on our current course and fail to reform our government policies, they may soon surpass us.

Ivory-towered economists endlessly wonder what has been the formula for America's economic success. How is it that this nation has created so much wealth and prosperity in such a short time?

Our short answer to that question is: freedom and free enterprise. No other nation has allowed these two ideals to flourish with so few restrictions in this century as the United States. The model is one of limited government, low taxes, protection of private-property rights, basic political rights and freedoms, free trade of goods and services, and the import of human capital through the immigration of talented, enterprising, and productive people. Throughout this century, the combination of a free people and free institutions—the "freedom solution," as Majority Leader Dick Armey calls it—has propelled America to new heights of prosperity.

Why then does it seem the American Dream is slipping away from so many of our citizens these days? Do freedom and free enterprise no longer pay dividends as they did earlier in this century?

We believe that it is precisely the gradual departure from these ideals over the past quarter century that has weakened the American economy. Indeed, the facts show that as the government has grown larger, the economy has grown more slowly. Since the early 1970s when government really started to explode in size, Americans' incomes haven't risen at all. In 1993 the median family income was $36,959—only slightly

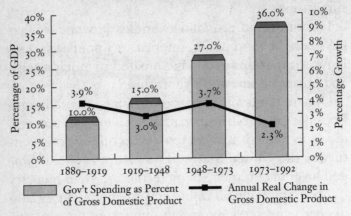

As Washington Grows, the Economy Slows

(Source: Institute for Policy Innovation, Lewisville, Texas, 1995)

higher than in 1973, $36,893 (calculated in 1993 dollars). Incomes fell drastically in the late 1970s, the Carter years; grew rapidly during the Reagan expansion of the 1980s, eclipsing the previous peak; but have been falling again in the high tax-and-spend 1990s.

What this suggests is that we have paid a heavy price for the big government that we have installed in Washington. Our well-intentioned efforts to create economic security for all have allowed us to depart from the basic principles that enhance economic well-being and financial security in the first place.

GOVERNMENT: THE SOLUTION OR THE PROBLEM?

In Washington, our critics have often mocked our general faith in free-market institutions to solve social problems. Those who have spent their entire careers building bureaucratic empires in Washington are loath to accept the notion that these institutions have actually become roadblocks to the American Dream. Our view from inside Congress is that there is much truth to the barb that big government is the opiate of the Washington intelligentsia. They are addicted to spending your money.

But curiously enough, more and more Americans recognize that our federal government has become more of a problem than a solution. A 1995 poll revealed devastating findings for supporters of centralized command-and-control solutions. In the poll the public was asked whether "government policies help or hinder you in trying to achieve the American Dream?" Thirty-one percent said such policies helped; 56 percent said they hindered. Here is what we found particularly striking about the survey. *Even Americans receiving public assistance—by a margin of 47-to-36 percent—believe government is more of a hindrance than a help in attaining the American Dream.*

We have identified eleven great bureaucratic structures in Washington that undercut the American Dream today:

1. A welfare system that cheats the poor, undermines the family, discourages marriage, and rewards undesirable behavior.
2. A failing public school system, funded increasingly with federal tax dollars and regulated by federal officials, that set-

tles for mediocrity and promotes the interests of bureaucrats and teacher unions over the interests of children.

3. A tax code that is anti-work, anti-investment, anti-savings, and anti-success.

4. A sprawling and hugely expensive federal bureaucracy that serves no one's interest but its own.

5. A vast and unaccountable federal regulatory structure that is smothering our private entrepreneurs, businesses, and workers.

6. An archaic legal system that has become far and away the most expensive in the world and acts as a millstone around the neck of our economy.

7. An anti-family mindset that permeates almost all of Washington's social, regulatory, tax, and welfare policies.

8. A government incapable of performing even its most vital function of keeping criminals in jail and out of our neighborhoods.

9. A health-care system whose costs are doubling every seven years and threatens to bankrupt our government.

10. A Washington Establishment that tries to cultivate within our citizens its corrupting creed of entitlement, dependency, and victimization over America's traditional ethic of work, responsibility, and opportunity.

11. A nearly $5 trillion debt that is eroding
America's ability to save, invest, and compete in a globally competitive marketplace. This debt is unquestionably
America's greatest moral and economic
crisis.

The mission that confronts us is clear. We in Congress,
in partnership with all citizens, must work with a unifying national purpose to resolve each of these problems. We simply cannot meet the global challenges of
the next century if our own government is working
against us.

AMERICANS IN PURSUIT OF THE DREAM

To understand how our $1.6 trillion government in
Washington builds roadblocks to the American Dream,
let's examine the plight of a hypothetical middle-
income family today.

John and Jane Smithson of Toledo, Ohio, aspire to
make a better life for themselves and their children.
John has a small carpentry business. Jane is a sales
assistant at a local bank. They both work hard at their
jobs; they make their house payments; they diligently
save for their son and daughter's college educations;
they give money to their church and local charities.
They strive each day to make sacrifices for their two
young children. And, like so many Americans these
days, they worry at times about making ends meet—
paying the endless stream of bills each month.

Each year as April 15 approaches, they spend about twenty hours of drudgery rummaging through their financial records to figure out how much they owe Uncle Sam. When they're through, if they're brave enough to look, they discover that they have turned over about 25 percent of their family budget to the government. (Next year, they resolve, they won't bother to look.) They're frustrated to learn that one-quarter of everything they work for is sent five hundred miles away to Washington—where they see little tangible return.

State and local taxes take another 15 percent off the Smithsons' income. This doesn't make them too angry; at least they can observe some return in services provided from those tax dollars.

In all, a whopping 40 percent of the Smithsons' earnings—money that could otherwise be saved, reinvested in John's fledgling business, or spent on the children—is siphoned off by government. That 40 percent is slightly more than they spend on food, housing, and clothing combined. One thing the Smithsons are certain of: they are nowhere near getting their money's worth from government.

But the government isn't through with the Smithsons yet. You see, the Smithsons also pay an enormous, hidden tab for unnecessary government rules and regulations. These costs are hidden in the price of the goods and services the Smithsons buy each day. Government regulation and frivolous litigation add approximately 10 percent to the cost of everything we buy. Regulation is like a hidden sales tax—and is just as regressive. So now, about 50 percent of the Smithsons' income is paid directly or indirectly to government.

Like so many honest and hard working Americans, the Smithsons innocently wonder: why is it so hard to achieve the American Dream these days?

But wait! There's one last item: the Smithsons' share of the national debt and the budget deficit. John and Jane Smithson each inherit about $75,000 of costs over their lifetime just to pay the interest on the debt. But they get off easy compared to their kids. Thanks to the iron law of compound interest, over their lifetimes the children will pay about $180,000 each in taxes to pay the interest on the debt. The Smithsons may be trying their best to build a better, more prosperous future for the children. But Uncle Sam surely is not. The Smithsons are exemplary and loving parents, but they can't undo the financial injustice that the government is inflicting upon their children.

THE ROBBER BARONS OF THE AMERICAN DREAM

The Smithsons' situation is not unique. They are discovering what most Americans already know is true: that when it comes to pursuing the American Dream, our overweight, irresponsible federal government has become a major deterrent. Let's examine in some detail the ways that Washington's policies have become the robber barons of the Dream:

The Crushing Tax Burden

The average American family now works 125 days of the year—through May 5—just to pay taxes. That's nearly $20,000 a year of the family budget that is sent to Washington to feed the government budget. In fact, the nonpartisan Washington-based Tax Foundation reports that, at 40 percent, taxes have now become the largest component of the typical middle-income family budget, followed by housing (15.5 percent), food (10 percent), medical care (10 percent), recreation (5 percent), and clothing (4 percent). When indirect taxes, such as taxes on businesses, are included, some families in high-tax states can pay close to half of their income in taxes. When the government leaves just over half of a family's income to spend on a home or a business or investment in children, it is a major impediment to the American Dream.

The National Debt

The nearly $5 trillion national debt hangs like an albatross around America's neck. The average family of four now inherits a $75,000 share of this debt. This is like carrying a second mortgage. Of course, when the government borrows more through deficit spending, there is a smaller pool of savings available for private investment. The deficit now absorbs about two-thirds of private savings in America. A standard rule of thumb is that the debt adds about 2 percentage points to interest rates in the United States. These higher interest rates add about $37,000 to the cost of an average thirty-year mortgage and about $900 more on a four-year loan for a new car. Worse yet, a worker born today inherits a lifetime of nearly $200,000 of tax payments just to pay federal interest payments.

It has been a long and honored tradition in America that parents paid off the mortgage and left their children the farm. Nowadays, we seem to be selling the farm and leaving our children the mortgage. That's hardly consistent with the American Dream.

Regulation

Federal regulations cost the economy an estimated $500 billion a year. That's almost 10 percent of our nearly $6.5 trillion national income. A typical household loses more than $5,000 a year due to regulation. These costs have roughly doubled after adjusting for inflation over the past twenty years. But because these are invisible costs, the federal regulator silently threatens the future of the American Dream.

Wasteful Federal Spending

Every opinion poll in recent years has come to the same conclusion: Americans don't think they're getting their money's worth from Washington. In a 1994 Luntz survey, Americans were asked, "How many cents do you think are wasted out of every dollar that government spends?" The answers were hardly a ringing endorsement for the value of government programs. Three out of four Americans believe that government wastes *at least* 25 cents of every dollar spent. Nearly four in ten believe that more than 50 cents of every federal dollar is wasted. Americans clearly think that they can spend their tax dollars better than Washington can. Given what we've seen dur-

ing our time in Washington, and the way federal bureaucrats will spend $1.6 trillion in 1995, we wholeheart-
edly agree. When Washington's waste costs every family
in America more in taxes, it cheats them of their wages
and reduces their opportunity to share in the American Dream.

A Failing School System

Education is a key stepping stone to achieving the
American Dream. To restore economic opportunity in
America and to maintain a high-wage, globally competitive work force, we need to ensure that our children are receiving the best education in the world.
Today, they are not. Amazingly, we are now spending
nearly $100,000 on the education of the average child
passing through our public school system from kinder-
garten through high school. This is more than any
other nation in the world spends. Yet we rank near the
bottom of industrial nations by almost every measure
of achievement—particularly in the areas of math and
science. Time and time again, national studies on the
state of our schools say that at best we are achieving
mediocrity. When our public school system hands
eighteen-year-olds diplomas they can't even read, we
are robbing them of almost any opportunity to succeed
and prosper in today's competitive world economy.

Cities of Despair

The American Dream has always been about offering the very poorest and most disadvantaged among

us the fullest opportunity to climb to the top rungs of the economic ladder of success. There are so many inspiring stories throughout our history—stories of Americans rising up from meager beginnings to achieve greatness in this land of opportunity. One of these success stories is Andrew Grove, who came to the United States from Cuba with only the clothes on his back. He is now the cofounder and CEO of Intel Corp., a $5 billion-a-year microchip producer and a proud symbol of America's technological leadership in the world.

But for mostly disadvantaged minorities growing up in our inner-city neighborhoods today—thanks to years of wrongheaded federal and urban policies—the path to the American Dream has become an obstacle course. Our inner cities have become the most over-taxed, overregulated, and overbureaucratized areas in America today. Uncle Sam has contributed to this cul-ture of public-sector paternalism. More than $2.5 tril-lion of federal tax dollars have been spent—or rather misspent—on our inner cities. That's the equivalent of twenty-five Marshall Plans. With this money we have erected massive public housing projects; we have pro-moted single-parenthood over marriage; we have installed a culture of welfare dependency; and we have subsidized school systems that don't teach.

So it should be no surprise that many of our once mighty industrial urban centers and the tens of mil-lions of Americans who live there are in greater finan-cial distress today than before this massive infusion of funds began. For too many years urban leaders in partnership with federal officials have created the poisonous ethic in cities that government, bureaucracy, and pity, rather than capitalism, freedom, and hope are the gateway to a better life. That ethic has been an enemy of the American Dream.

The Welfare State

Welfare began as a well-intentioned safety net for the poorest among us. As with so much of what we try to do in Washington, those good intentions have gone terribly awry. Nothing has eroded the American Dream for so many of our citizens more insidiously than the $5 trillion modern welfare state. The welfare state seems almost designed to destroy the institution of fatherhood in America today. It seems designed to erode the work ethic. It seems designed to trap Americans in a cycle of dependency, rather than to encourage individual responsibility.

There is no single trend in America today more worrisome to us than the rise in illegitimacy. It's happening among all races. Thirty years ago 7.7 percent of babies were born out of wedlock. Today it's 28 percent. Make no mistake about it, if this trend is not broken and reversed, the American Dream will simply cease to exist. When we pay a seventeen-year-old girl to have a baby out of wedlock, we are almost certainly slamming the door on her chance to pursue a rewarding and productive adult life. Even more tragically, when we help create a society of fatherless homes, we are doing a great and ignoble disservice to the children.

PREPARING GOVERNMENT FOR THE INFORMATION AGE

How can we fix our government so that it no longer collides with Americans' dreams and aspirations? One answer is that we need to learn the lessons of our private industries and entrepreneurs. If government will follow the lead of the productivity revolution in the private sector, we can accomplish dramatic improvements in the service and cost-effectiveness of our institutions in Washington.

Despite virtually all the handicaps that Washington imposes on our businesses and our workers, American industries are reengineering themselves to win in the global marketplace. A headline from *The Washington Post* reported in late 1994 that DOWNSIZED FIRMS PRODUCE MORE WITH LESS. According to the story, "The driving force behind the economic expansion has been a productivity revolution that has rolled through industry after industry, forcing companies to merge and downsize and alter nearly every aspect of the way they do business to produce more with less."

The story is the same throughout the private sector. We are now witnessing a breathtaking restructuring of American industry. Our semiconductor industry, for example, after facing several years of worrisome market penetration from the Japanese, is once again world dominant. Our pharmaceutical and biotechnology industries continue to be first in developing almost every single wonder drug of the modern era. Of the fifty breakthrough drugs of the last fifteen years, forty-

five of them were developed in the United States—
all of this despite the impediments at the Food and
Drug Administration.

Perhaps the most unlikely of success stories is the
comeback of the once moribund American steel industry. Fifteen years ago this domestic industry was being
buried by cheap imported steel and teetering on the
brink of bankruptcy. Today, thanks to a major restructuring of such steel producers as American Iron and
Steel, domestic demand is up, profits are hitting record
levels, and American producers are witnessing a surging export market, as they try to keep up with foreign
demand for U.S. steel.

Imagine if we could accomplish the same turnaround
in the operations of our government. Here, then, are
some of the lessons that these and other economic
winners can teach us in Washington about how to compete and succeed:

Bureaucracy Is Dead

The world is in the midst of an information revolution; archaic, bureaucratic structures are giving way
to modern communications technologies and pro-
cesses. Think of the speed and ease with which we
use a bank teller card anywhere in the country to get
cash or verify our checking-account balance. Now contrast that situation with the frustrations of trying to
obtain information from the Social Security Administration, the Internal Revenue Service, or even Congress
itself. John Roach, president of Tandy Corp., thinks
that the problem with government today is excessive

bureaucracy. "Businesses have been restructuring for the last decade," he points out. "Now it's time for the government to start."

Productivity Drives Results

We need to recognize the reality of the global market: to create American jobs through world sales and to have the jobs that pay the highest wages, we have to have the highest productivity. Japan, Germany, Taiwan, Korea, and, now the world's next great competitor, China, have been doing this and are rapidly catching up to us.

American industries recognize the challenge and have been aggressively meeting the competition and winning. Ford Motor Company, for example, has undergone a remarkable transition from near-financial insolvency to the very paragon of sound fiscal health and profitability. In 1994 Ford had record profits of $5.3 billion. It's starting to beat Honda and Toyota in many markets. What is the secret of Ford's success? Today Ford produces a Taurus with two and one-half times the quality but only one-half the workforce required fifteen years ago. *Business Week* magazine recently surveyed the performance of American firms in more than a dozen industries over the period 1990–94. *Business Week* discovered that the industries that are succeeding are doing two things: they are reducing their bureaucracies and increasing their output per worker. Eight key industries have dramatically increased in a four-year period their productivity per worker: steel (29 percent), chemicals (17 percent), computers (152 percent), semiconductors (83 percent), telecommunications (33 percent), energy (20 percent), banking (12 percent), autos (18 percent).

How does this compare with the bureaucratic structure of the public sector? Today, government in America has about 500,000 more employees than our entire manufacturing sector. Industry is producing more with less. Government is producing less with more.

Modern Economies Are Driven by Knowledge and Skills

As we move further into an information and computer age, the premium on education, skills, and expertise is rising rapidly. Across the globe, there is no shortage of unskilled labor. Today our businesses seek knowledgeable, inventive minds. In 1993 the median income for a high-school graduate was $15,000; for a college graduate, $27,500; for a person with a master's degree, $36,000; and for a holder of a Ph.D., $48,000. These differentials have been widening over time. The implications are obvious: knowledge and skills are the gateway to economic success.

Wealth and Capital Know No Boundaries

In the information age, where goods, services, and information can be transmitted across the globe at the speed of light, arbitrary national boundaries are no obstacle to wealth and capital. This means that the essence of liberalism—Robin Hood income-redistribution policies—are becoming futile. Wealth can't be confiscated in an information age; it must be created. The Asian "tigers" of Japan, Korea, Hong Kong, Taiwan, and others know this. European nations, such as Sweden, that for years became entirely oriented toward egalitarianism and income redistribution, are rapidly discarding such economic policies as unaffordable and defunct. We must now do the same.

The Keys to Success Are Modernization and Innovation

Productive and profitable firms in America ask the practical question: what works and what doesn't? They experiment; they learn; they modernize; they reform themselves. Those that don't perish. Consider the computer microchip industry. Moore's law, named after Intel cofounder Gordon Moore, says that the number of transistors crammed onto a microchip doubles every eighteen months. An IBM PC offers 1,000 times more computing power than the same machine sold at the same price six years ago. Any semiconductor firm that falls just a few months behind its competitors is out of business.

This kind of hyper-innovation is an entirely alien concept in government. If government had been as productive as the microchip industry over the past thirty years, it would now have just four workers and a budget of $100,000. These are the kinds of frontiers of progress we should be thinking about in government.

How far behind is the government in adapting to the information age? The sad truth is that our federal government doesn't even recognize in some cases that the microchip exists. For example, today the Federal Aviation Administration uses vacuum tubes in the air traffic control system that routes planes and keeps us safe from collisions. This is hundred-year-old technology. Because of bureaucratic and complicated government purchasing rules, our government has not been able in seven years to figure out how to replace vacuum tubes with a microchip that has the computing power of 3 million vacuum tubes.

THE FREEDOM SOLUTION

How do we apply these lessons from the private sector? Clearly we have a mighty challenge ahead. Our government is still operating with a 1950s mindset as we enter the twenty-first century. This means we have to transform our government—to change the way it thinks, the way it does business, the way it serves its customers (the taxpayers) to prepare it for the information age.

To do so, we must start by laying out the concrete goals we wish to achieve through this bold transformation. Certainly we can forge a bipartisan consensus over the goals. Here are the primary goals we have established for twenty-first century government:

• A permanently balanced budget with a *declining* national debt.

• Schools that inspire children to learn and are safe.

- An urban renewal in America that empowers even the most disadvantaged citizens.

- Replacement of the welfare state with an opportunity society.

- A lean, cost-efficient, and less-intrusive federal enterprise.

- The best system of health care in the world, accessible to all.

- A civil society that depends more on the goodwill of our citizens than the decrees of government.

- A pro-entrepreneur, pro-science and technology, pro-savings economy that produces the best products in the world.

- Job opportunities with high wages for all Americans.

- Security at home and abroad.

- A heightened respect for the genius of the American Constitution.

OUR VISION FOR CHANGE

With the *Contract*, we're off to a promising start in taking back our government. Many of the steps we took in our *Contract with America* were designed to help combat the deficiencies of the institutions in Washington. But now we need to complete the transition we began in January 1995.

Here are the next eight specific items that we propose to accomplish:

1. Pass a budget that ends deficit spending.

We will propose and pass a federal budget that eliminates deficit spending by 2002 and does not raise a penny of new taxes. This will be the first budget to pass Congress in twenty-five years that lays out a path to a balanced budget.

2. Enact budget reforms that keep Congress on the balanced-budget track.

We will continue to press for a balanced budget amendment, but in the meantime, we will pass and enforce a legislative balanced budget requirement that by law keeps Congress on the path to a zero deficit by 2002.

3. Eliminate and consolidate Cabinet agencies.

We will eliminate at least three of the fourteen Cabinet agencies and substantially reorganize another five. The agencies that will undergo this dramatic restructuring include the Department of Energy, the

Education Department, the Department of Housing
and Urban Development, the Commerce Department, the Labor Department, and the Department
of Agriculture.

4. Replace the welfare state with an opportunity society.

We will continue to turn over most major welfare
program and funding responsibilities to the states while
offering them flexibility to reform the system as they
see fit. The states are already far ahead of Washington in devising innovative and effective alternatives
to welfare. Welfare cannot be fixed; it must be replaced
entirely with an opportunity-society agenda.

5. Reduce health-care costs and prevent
Medicare's insolvency.

The Medicare system, which provides health care
security for 32 million senior citizens and 4 million
disabled people to prevent impending bankruptcy, is
on the critical list. Medicare trustees, who include
three Clinton Cabinet members, have warned that it
will go bankrupt in 2002. We will fill the leadership
gap left in the wake of President Clinton's steadfast
silence on this impending crisis, and we will save Medicare for our senior citizens and for our children.

We believe health-care reform worthy of the name
must reduce costs, maintain quality, secure access, and
provide choice of doctors. We will pass a health-care

reform bill that rejects a Clinton-style government takeover of medicine and instead maximizes individual choices, insures that no child or family member can be denied coverage because of a preexisting condition, and provides for continuity of coverage for Americans who fear losing their health insurance if they lose or change jobs, move, or get sick.

6. Forge a new partnership with our cities.

We will not desert our cities. To bring capital and businesses back to urban America, we will pursue various options, including an eighteen-month "time out" on all federal mandates imposed on cities, expanded school choice options for parents with children in failed inner-city school systems, making federally designated enterprise zones in the most depressed areas of our cities zero capital gains tax centers, and reducing taxes on families in cities.

7. Simplify and reform our anti-competitive tax system.

We want to move toward replacing the current 1,400-page Internal Revenue code. We've asked former Rep. Jack Kemp to chair a commission to examine the best way to simplify taxes and reward investment. We expect to have a recommendation within the next few months.

8. Slash the bloated bureaucracy in Washington.

Our budget reduction proposals will involve a dramatic reduction of wasteful, bureaucratic, and redundant programs in Washington. For the first time in many years, we will prove that Congress can do more than just start programs—we can end them as well. After our first year in control, we will have eliminated at least fifty programs that have outlived their original missions, assuming they ever had any in the first place. All of these efforts will be designed to create in Washington a more cost-effective, citizen-responsive, flexible, twenty-first century government. Our goal is to unleash the boundless talents and energies of our people and businesses by ending fifty years of bureaucratic micromanagement in Washington.

A GOVERNMENT OF, BY, AND FOR THE PEOPLE

Clearly, our $1.6 trillion government doesn't know how to adapt, modernize, or innovate. It is a dinosaur: slow, cumbersome, inefficient, and outdated. It's not up to the challenges of the information age. It mostly pursues its own interests of self-preservation, not the public interest of providing quality services at low cost. Our goal and mission over the next eighteen months is to topple the exhausted bureaucratic regime in Washington. Our reforms are meant to literally reengineer our government just as private industry has done so prudently and effectively over the past ten years. We believe such reforms are a necessary first step in restoring the American Dream.

3

The Moral Imperative for a Balanced Budget

AFTER MORE THAN twenty-five years of deficit spending in Washington, isn't it finally time that Congress balance the budget? Nineteen sixty-nine—that's the year that should be indelibly etched in the minds of every American. It's the last time Uncle Sam balanced his spending with his receipts. Four-and-a-half trillion dollars of debt later, Americans can only conclude that deficit spending is consuming us and that it will bankrupt our nation unless we change course. Without change, our fiscal future looks grim. According to President Clinton's own budget forecast, we are condemned to year after year of ever-rising tidal waves of debt for as far as the eye can see. This debt is poisoning our economy, our children's future, and our moral resolve as a nation to confront and conquer a great crisis.

Back in 1936 President Franklin Delano Roosevelt made his famous pronouncement to the nation that "this generation of Americans has a rendezvous with destiny." The destiny of that generation of Americans was to defeat Nazi Germany and Imperial Japan in the Second World War. Many prior and subsequent generations of Americans have experienced a "rendezvous with destiny." The destiny of our Founding Fathers, the first generation to call themselves "Americans," was to give birth to this free nation founded on the revolutionary notion that all men are created equal and endowed with basic inalienable rights of life, liberty, and the pursuit of happiness. Another generation fought a great and bloody war to end the evil of slavery and preserve the Union. Another fought and defeated the Germans in the First World War. Most recently, a generation of Americans, through military, economic, and moral might, vanquished the communist menace—the greatest threat to the freedom of nations in the second half of the twentieth century.

The greatness of America and Americans has been our ability to unflinchingly confront every national crisis that has arisen before us. Throughout our nation's history, every generation, with a steely moral resolve and a unifying national commitment, has triumphed over every major crisis. Their sacrifices were made for the good of their country and to ensure a free and prosperous future for their children.

Today, our generation of Americans is now confronting one of those historic moments. We need to choose whether we will regain control of our nation's economic destiny, whether we will balance the budget, or whether we will borrow against the future.

To us, the choice is clear. Our nation has a duty to balance the federal budget—and keep it balanced. We want to describe why a balanced budget is a moral, patriotic, and economically vital national commitment.

AMERICA'S RED INK NIGHTMARE

For thousands of years, great and wise leaders have warned against the economic calamity of continuous government deficit spending. Throughout history, many of the great empires of Western civilization have suffered the fate of taxing, spending, and borrowing themselves to death. As far back as 63 B.C., Cicero, one of Rome's greatest orators and statesmen, issued advice to his fellow citizens that seems well-suited to contemporary America: "The budget should be balanced; the treasury should be refilled; public debt should be repaid . . . lest Rome become bankrupt."

Through most of America's history, our citizens and our elected leaders in Washington have resisted the political temptation of paying for government spending through debt. In fact, until 1930—or through the first 150 years of this nation's history—the federal government routinely ran budget *surpluses*. Total federal government spending consumed less than 4 percent of national output (compared to 22 percent today). There was a moral, if not a constitutional, imperative that the federal government pay its bills and avoid passing the buck to future generations. The only general exception to this moral rule was that it was deemed appropriate for the national government to borrow during times of war—often by issuing war bonds. Yet, once the war was over, Americans demanded that Washington not only return to a balanced budget, but even retire the wartime debt by running surpluses. For example, during the First World War, the federal government ran up a $20 billion debt. By 1928, within ten years of the armistice, more than one-third of the debt had been repaid.

Nobel Prize–winning economist James M. Buchanan, of George Mason University, has explained how this prevailing fiscal discipline was enforced politically. "Balanced budgets were dictated by moral standards," he observed, even though they were never "explicitly mentioned in formal constitutional documents." This long-held and prudent moral imperative began to dissolve for the first time during the Great Depression. At about that time the most prominent economist of the first half of the twentieth century, John Maynard Keynes, introduced his controversial economic theory, which effectively embraced deficit financing as an appropriate tool of government. Keynes believed that government should borrow when times were tough and then pay back the debt during times of economic expansion. President Roosevelt was the first President to embrace this theory, which fit well with his New Deal domestic-spending aspirations.

It is worth noting that, from the start, the intellectually appealing theory of using government deficit financing to stimulate the economy never worked well in practice, and it certainly failed under FDR. During the 1930s, when the New Deal was launched, federal spending tripled in dollar terms and doubled as a share of national output. But by 1940, after years of record peacetime deficits, the Great Depression dragged on. It was the transition toward a wartime economy in 1941, not peacetime deficits, that ended the Depression. If deficits stimulated economic growth, America would be in the midst of a roaring prosperity today. Adjusted for inflation, the 1990s have recorded the largest peacetime deficits ever.

By stripping away the prevailing moral restraint against government borrowing, Keynes opened the floodgate for massive deficit spending. Once the genie was out of the bottle, it was impossible to stuff it back in. By 1970 Richard Nixon would declare "we are all Keynesians now." Government red ink would soon explode to once unimaginable levels as each subsequent Congress used more and more debt as a way of handing out political favors and subsidies, without having to pay the bill. Deficit spending became the ultimate free lunch. The philosophy was one of spend today, pay later—preferably long after we've left office.

With each passing decade Washington became increasingly hooked on deficit spending. We now borrow during times of war and times of peace; during good times and bad. The fiscal deterioration in Washington has been swift and terrible. Consider these depressing facts:

• From the time of George Washington's inauguration through 1963 the federal government recorded a total net deficit of $250 billion in 1963 dollars. In 1993 alone, the annual deficit reached $255 billion. In other words, the federal government borrowed more money in 1993 alone than it did in the entire first 180 years of our nation's history.

• Uncle Sam now borrows $650 million each and every day. Think of how many homes could be purchased, schools built, small businesses financed, pot-holes filled, and new factories opened with $650 million. Heck, with $650 million, we could buy 10,000 Americans a brand new Mercedes-Benz convertible—each and every day of the year.

• According to the Third Millennium, an organization of young Americans, the typical American taxpayer must work two-and-a-half months of the year just to pay for Congress's annual deficit spending. If we could eliminate the budget deficit by cutting spending, every American in the labor force could work seventy-five fewer days of the year for Uncle Sam and seventy-five days more for themselves and their families.

• If we were to try to pay off the $4.8 trillion national debt by having Congress put one dollar every second into a special debt reduction account, how many years would it take to pay off the debt? One million seconds is about twelve days. One billion seconds is roughly thirty-two years. But one trillion seconds is almost 32,000 years. So if Congress put dollar bills into this account for about the next 160,000 years—or roughly the amount of time that has passed since the Ice Age—the debt would be paid off.

TAXATION WITHOUT REPRESENTATION

Of course, the real burden of the national debt will be borne by our children and our children's children. This is precisely why Americans once held a deeply ingrained moral taboo against deficit spending. Budget deficits are the ultimate form of what our nation was founded to protect against: taxation without representation.

Consider the situation of Eric Klawitter, living in Arlington Heights, Illinois. Eric isn't particularly interested in politics. He doesn't have much of a voice at the table in Washington over federal budget decisions. He doesn't even vote. And no one ever asked him whether we should have wool and mohair subsidies, urban transit grants, or welfare payments to alcoholics and drug addicts. In fact, he doesn't have the slightest idea of what any of these things are. But then, Eric is only three-years-old. One thing is certain, however. Eric may not have voted for a dime of today's deficit spending programs, but twenty years from now, he will share in the financial burden of paying for all of them.

We hear our critics in Washington talk endlessly about tax fairness. But we would ask these skeptics—especially those Democrats in the Senate who blocked the passage of the balanced budget amendment—a simple question: Where is the fairness in requiring a three-year-old to pay taxes tomorrow for the excesses of government today? Who in Washington, among the thousands of powerful special-interest lobbyists and self-proclaimed do-gooders, speaks for the children who will have to pay off our irresponsible debts? Of course, there are groups like the Children's Defense Fund and the National Education Association who daily proclaim that they represent the best interests of children. But do they really? Both these groups lobbied furiously *against* the balanced budget amendment.

We think it's plainly obvious that the single most pro-child policy that any of us can pursue is to reduce the crushing burden of debt our government is now placing on the next generation's backs.

HOW THE DEFICIT AFFECTS YOU AND ME

Of course, the tragedy of the $4.8 trillion dollar national debt is that we don't have to wait thirty, twenty, or even ten years to feel its impact on our lives. The crisis is already here—it's right at our doorstep. One way that the deficit affects us is by making an ever-larger claim on our tax dollars. Today, 41 cents out of every income tax dollar that Americans send to Washington is devoted exclusively to paying the interest on the debt. When we include the interest payments owed to the Social Security program and other trust funds, the interest payment rises to a staggering 62 cents of every personal income tax dollar.

Interest on the debt is now the third largest component of the federal budget behind Social Security and national defense. Interest now costs us $225 billion a year. By 1997, we will be paying more for interest than for our entire army, navy, marine corps, and air force combined. By then, we will be paying an estimated $257 billion for national defense, and a whopping $270 billion for interest on the national debt.

How do these massive interest payments affect the average American worker? Let's examine the case of three hypothetical Americans: Robert R. born in 1959, Mary N. born in 1974, and Sally C. born in 1995. Here is how much each of these workers will pay over their lifetime in taxes just to pay for interest:

	Year of birth	Interest paid over 75 years
Robert R.	1959	$75,851
Mary N.	1974	$115,724
Sally C.	1995	$187,150

Robert will work more than a year to pay for the deficit. Mary will work roughly two whole years of her life to pay her share. And Sally, who was born this year, will work nearly a month and a half every year of her entire working life just to pay for the deficit. This is the very definition of "money for nothing."

IS OUR GOVERNMENT BANKRUPT?

Can this federal addiction to red ink go on forever? There is a simple rule of thumb in personal finance that a family's debt charges should never exceed 15 percent of its income. If they do, according to *The New York Times Personal Finance Handbook*, then "the family is overextended." Using this rule of thumb, how can the government's finances shape up? The federal government's interest payments now comprise 17 percent of its income (i.e., tax receipts). This insolvency ratio may soon rise to close to 20 percent.

The runaway national debt has much the same impact on our nation's financial condition as termites do on the structure of a house. Termites gradually and secretly chomp away at the foundation of a house and continually weaken its entire structure. For a long time termites leave no immediate visible sign of damage to the home's foundation. It is as if they were not there. But once the damage has been done, woe to the home-owner! The cost of fixing the damage is painfully high. It would have been much cheaper if, early on, the termites had been exterminated.

And so it is with our budget deficit. The economic foundation that the deficit is eroding is our pool of national savings. None of us readily notice the impact, but the dirty work is being done at this very moment. Government borrowing consumed 2 percent of net private savings in the 1960s; 10 percent in the 1970s; 40 percent in the 1980s; and nearly 70 percent by the mid-1990s.

Why does this matter? Because our stock of savings is a basic building block for a productive national economy. We need savings to finance investment, to build new homes and factories, purchase new computers and farm tractors, and open new schools and training centers. These investments are what raise the productivity of American workers and ultimately lead to higher living standards.

Not surprisingly, given Uncle Sam's $4.8 trillion debt, America's national savings rate is well below that of our international competitors. In 1993 and 1994 America had a 4.1 percent savings rate, the lowest two years since the end of the Second World War. This compares with a savings rate of about 14 percent for Japan and 11 percent for Germany.

A basic ingredient to achieving the American Dream is thrift. When we engage in thrift by saving our money, we are essentially delaying gratification. But today for every three dollars that Americans save, the government borrows two. By hijacking our savings, the government hijacks our opportunity to experience the American Dream.

THE IMMORALITY OF THE "PARTY-ON" APPROACH

To be perfectly honest, we would love to keep playing Santa Claus. We could pretend the debt doesn't exist; pass out $1.6 trillion of government largesse each year, and let the next Congress deal with the rising sea of red ink. This would certainly endear us to most groups in Washington—and even to many of our constituents who benefit directly from this or that government program. In our profession, the politics of giving is always more popular than the politics of taking away.

Regrettably, this is precisely the approach the President has chosen with his most recent budget plan. In what we regard as a spectacular abdication of leadership, the President's plan to deal with the deficit is to do—nothing. Even Labor Secretary Robert Reich conceded as much when he said during the balanced budget amendment debate that the "President is against simply balancing the budget." We dub this the Democrats' "party-on" strategy. That strategy is to keep spending and borrowing, and worry about the red ink tomorrow, or next week, or next year, or next decade.

Of course, President Clinton claims that thanks to his tax hike—the largest ever—the deficit crisis is subsiding. Oh, how we wish it were so. The facts are infinitely more discouraging. It is true that this year's deficit is down—but to a little less than $200 billion. The Congressional Budget Office forecasts a federal deficit of $284 billion in fiscal year 2000, $322 billion in 2002, and $383 billion in 2004. The cyclical fall in the deficit in 1995 has not lessened the magnitude of the longer-term emergency. To even hint that it has is the height of irresponsibility.

Because of the large increase expected in expenditures for federal health care, Social Security, civil service retirement, and other benefit programs—the so-called entitlements—the longer-term outlook is even bleaker. Recently, a blue-ribbon bipartisan commission—headed by Sen. Robert Kerrey, Democrat from Nebraska, and John Danforth, a former Republican senator from Missouri—examined the implications of the "business-as-usual" option. The report's findings are sobering and underscore the disastrous implications of "party-on" economics.

Kerrey and Danforth find that if we stay on our current fiscal path, the deficit will be about 11 percent of total national output (more than three times larger than today) by 2020, and 19 percent of national output by 2030 (six times larger than today). Then look what happens to the national debt under the Clinton "stay-the-course" option. By the end of 1995, our national debt is expected to be $4.8 trillion; five years later, by the turn of the century, it is projected at $6.4 trillion; by 2010, it will have almost doubled to $11.5 trillion. In other words, within the next ten years, the national debt will be larger than our current entire national income. President Clinton may be willing to live with that. We aren't.

GENERATIONAL INEQUITY

Of course, one option in dealing with the debt would be to just raise taxes to accommodate higher spending on entitlements in the future. To do that, we would have to nearly double every federal tax imposed on every family in America over the next twenty-five years. Somehow, we don't think our children—the future workers of America—are going to be comforted by that news.

Again, the picture gets bleaker as we move further into the future. President Clinton's first budget document explains the problem poignantly. It contains a table that lists the percentage of lifetime income that future generations of workers will pay in taxes. As government has grown over this century, this percentage has steadily risen from 24 percent in 1900 to an expected 36 percent for those born in 1992. For children born today and in the future, however, the continued expansion of government plus the huge cost of servicing the $5 trillion debt largely built up over the past twenty years push up this percentage to towering new heights.

Given the path we're on today, the share of lifetime earnings surrendered to taxes will reach 80 percent for future workers. In other words, 80 cents of every dollar earned by a child born today will go to pay taxes—most of which is to pay the bills on today's excessive spending.

THE BALANCED BUDGET AMENDMENT

The late great social scientist C. Northcote Parkinson, the scholar who coined "Parkinson's Law," once decried the growth of government deficit spending by declaring: "Without any conscious thought, the politicians have come to the conclusion that the interests of the next generation can be, and should be, ignored." He then asked of our lawmakers: "Can they not sense the disasters toward which they are heading? Can they not perceive what the future holds for them and for us?" For too many years now the answers to those questions have been, No, in Washington they cannot.

The destruction of our nation's once firmly held moral stricture against deficit spending requires us to amend our Constitution and command Congress to do what it used to feel honor-bound to do—balance the budget. A number-one priority of the 104th Congress will be to continue to push for passage of this vital twenty-eighth Amendment to the Constitution. In an historic, bipartisan vote in the House of Representatives in January, we obtained the two-thirds majority to pass the balanced budget amendment. In the Senate, however, it was politics as usual. The amendment was defeated by one vote when six Democratic senators switched their vote to no, thus handing the special-interest groups a triumphant victory over the American people—at least for the moment.

The argument was made by tax-and-spend opponents of this measure that a constitutional requirement for a balanced budget is just "a gimmick." Americans surely don't believe this. After all, if the amendment were a gimmick, Congress would have approved it long ago. The reason corporate lobbyists, federal workers, teachers unions, the welfare industry, and other powerful special-interest groups ferociously attacked the amendment is not because they think it won't work, but because they shudder at the thought that it will. What frightens the predator economy in Washington is that gift-bearing politicians may have the federal credit card taken away.

Another unconvincing argument made in defense of deficit spending is that "we owe the debt to ourselves." Unfortunately, we owe it increasingly to foreign interests. Foreign investors now own about $600 billion, or 15 percent, of the net national debt—a percentage that is rising. What this means is that our children owe much of the debt to Japan's children and Europe's children.

The American people have said in overwhelming numbers that they want the balanced budget amendment and intend to have it. The only real remaining question about the amendment is not if—*but when*—will it pass?

OUR PLEDGE TO BALANCE THE BUDGET

Whether a balanced budget amendment is approved this year or not, we regard the elimination of the deficit as our central mission. We recently asked Federal Reserve Chairman Alan Greenspan what he thought would be the impact of balancing the budget. He told us: "I think real incomes would significantly improve . . . Americans would look forward to their children doing better than they." In other words, it would be a major step toward restoring the American Dream.

Here is a pact that we wish to make with the Democrats in Congress, with the special-interest lobbies in Washington, with President Clinton, and especially with the American people: Starting immediately, let's work together in good faith and with all our collective wisdom to end the moral evil of deficit spending. Let's stop the blame game, the finger pointing, the multitude of excuses for why a balanced budget can't be achieved and why it's too hard. Let's all make a national commitment to ending this unconscionable system of fiscal abuse.

AMERICA'S DESTINY

The year is 2025. A grandmother is sitting with her two grandchildren bouncing on her lap. She is trying to explain to these toddlers what they probably cannot be made to understand. Why taxes are so enormously high. Why so many of America's formerly mighty industries are closing. Why there is so much economic dislocation. Why interest rates are sky-rocketing and the dollar buys so little. Why the United States, once an economic superpower, has managed to sink to seventh place, well behind Japan and Germany.

This could be America's destiny, but it won't be. We are sure of it. This generation of Americans—as with every generation before us—will meet the challenge of our historic moment. Our paramount responsibility is to balance the budget by ending the boundless growth of government. We will force our government to start doing what every industry in America has already found a way to do: grind out the waste and find ways to produce more with less.

We acknowledge that the job of balancing the budget is going to be the most difficult job for Congress to accomplish in decades. But in partnership with the American people, it will get done. This commitment we owe not just to our children, but equally to the generations of Americans who came before us and helped build this free and prosperous nation.

4
Returning to Fiscal Sanity

SHOULD WE BALANCE the federal budget by cutting bloated government spending or by taxing families first? That's the critical choice that confronts our nation. By now, if you're like most Americans, when you hear Washington politicians pontificating about deficit reduction, you probably shudder and grab for your wallet. That's understandable. In recent years, when the Democrats ran Congress, the term "deficit reduction" became synonymous with the words "tax increase." Congress raised taxes in 1980, 1982, 1983, 1984, 1987, 1988, 1990, and 1993. Typically, Americans were promised two dollars of spending reductions for every dollar of new taxes. In the end, we seemed to always get the taxes and never the promised spending cuts. When the Democrats talked about "sacrifice" they meant that taxpayers should sacrifice for the good of Washington.

Our approach is a radical departure from that strategy. We think Washington should do most of the sacrificing and the rest of America should reap the rewards. In other words, we intend to balance the budget so that we can increase, rather than plunder, the family budget. In fact, we will balance the budget and provide $200 billion of family and economic growth tax cuts. Our deficit problem is driven by too much spending in Washington, not too few tax dollars sent there.

OUR OUT-OF-CONTROL
FEDERAL BUDGET

How much has our federal budget expanded in recent decades? Here's a bit of historical perspective. In 1950, *Fortune* magazine ran a cover story with the ominous title: THE BUDGET IS OUT OF CONTROL! The article complained that "As if its sheer size and momentum had made it untouchable, nobody seems able to eliminate the waste that everybody recognizes." Then the article continued: "By any sane economics, Congress should . . . unmercifully sweat down the $42.4 billion that Mr. Truman plans to spend in the year ending July 1, 1951."

If a $42 billion budget was denounced as "out of control" forty-five years ago, then how are we to describe our budget of $1.6 trillion today? Even after adjusting for inflation, the federal budget is eight times larger today than it was in 1950 when *Fortune* complained of wasteful and excessive federal expenditures. In this century, the federal budget has risen from $8.3 billion to $1.6 trillion—after adjusting for inflation.

The Institute for Policy Innovation reports in its booklet *Government: America's Number 1 Growth Industry* that the federal government is now so large that in 1995 its expenditures will exceed the entire gross domestic products of nations such as Australia, Britain, China, France, Italy, and Spain. There are still two nations that have gross domestic products larger than the United States government: Germany and Japan. But lately Uncle Sam's budget has been growing faster than their economies.

Of course, the nation is much larger today than in earlier times, so one would expect government also to be bigger—though not disproportionately so. Even when adjusting for the growth in population size and inflation, government expenditures (in 1990 dollars) are three times higher than in 1950 and twice as high as in the early 1960s. Washington now spends roughly $15,000 for every household in America.

Few Americans think that services are twice as good today as they were before. In fact, most Americans complain that basic government services are much worse today than in the past. Indeed, it is no accident that as government has grown larger over the past four decades, there has been a steady erosion in the percentage of Americans who trust government to "do the right thing." In the 1960s, roughly 60 percent of Americans said they had confidence in government "most of the time." Today, less than 25 percent agree with this statement.

Even as a share of total economic output, government has ballooned to an unprecedented size. Federal spending consumed less than 5 percent of total output in 1900, 15 percent of total output in 1950, and is now about 22 percent of national output.

Look closely at the graph at the top of the next page. It shows the growth of federal spending and taxes over the last century. Federal taxes have rapidly increased, especially over the past thirty years. The problem has been that spending keeps accelerating at an even faster pace. Raising taxes to reduce the deficit is as futile as the greyhound trying to catch the mechanical rabbit at a dog race.

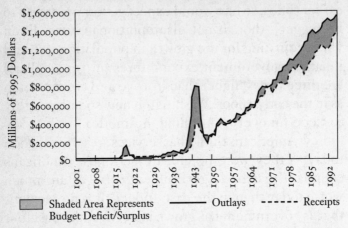

Real Federal Taxes and Spending, 1901–1995

(Source: *Budget of the U.S. Government*—Historical Tables, FY 1996; *Economic Report of the President*, February 1995)

If Congress had shown even an inclination toward spending restraint in recent years, our national debt nightmare might not exist today. If federal outlays had been restrained to just the general rate of inflation over the past twenty years, America would now have a $200 billion budget surplus, instead of a $200 billion deficit. Ronald Reagan was right when he said that to compare the spending habits of Congress with drunken sailors was unfair to drunken sailors.

DID DEFENSE SPENDING CAUSE THE DEFICIT?

Probably the most enduring myth of the 1980s is that the Reagan defense buildup was responsible for the growth of the budget deficit. The truth is that only about 40 cents of every dollar of spending increases in the 1980s was attributable to the Reagan defense buildup. From 1980 through 1992, real Pentagon spending climbed by roughly $60 billion, but real domestic spending grew by $220 billion.

Let's take the longer view for a moment. When we do we make a startling discovery. Pentagon spending could hardly be said to be responsible for our debt crisis, because national defense spending now constitutes a lower share of our budget than at any time in two hundred years! In the first federal budget, almost three-quarters of all expenditures were for the army and navy. Throughout our history, defense spending has averaged roughly half of federal spending. What is the percentage today? Just 20 percent. And that percentage is expected to drop to 15 percent by the year 2000.

We certainly want to eliminate waste in the Pentagon budget whenever and wherever we find it. But the evidence is clear that it is the hemorrhaging of domestic programs—not national defense—that has bloated our budget in Washington.

AMERICA'S ENTITLEMENT MENTALITY

Where is all this avalanche of spending going? Almost all domestic programs are growing, but none faster than entitlements. Reining in the entitlement ethic in America is going to be perhaps the single greatest political challenge that confronts us. We have created such a universal entitlement mentality in the United States that the rarity these days is to find an American who is *not* "entitled" to cash or services from the federal government. Each month the federal government sends out tens of billions of dollars to farmers, veterans, the unemployed, the poor, college students, the elderly, unwed mothers, the sick, and even very healthy and wealthy corporations. The practical political problem with controlling the cost of these programs is that, as George Bernard Shaw once noted: "A government which robs Peter to pay Paul can always count on Paul's support."

Entitlements are gobbling up a larger share of the budget pie every year. The charts on this and the facing page were compiled by the Kerrey-Danforth commission on entitlements. It found that mandatory spending (entitlements and interest on the debt) consumed about 30 percent of the budget in 1963, but about twice that share, or about 60 percent, by 1993.

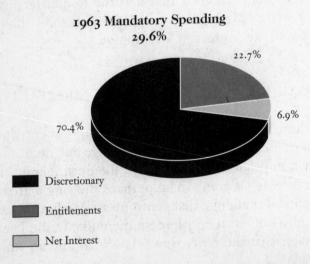

1963 Mandatory Spending
29.6%

22.7%

6.9%

70.4%

■ Discretionary

■ Entitlements

□ Net Interest

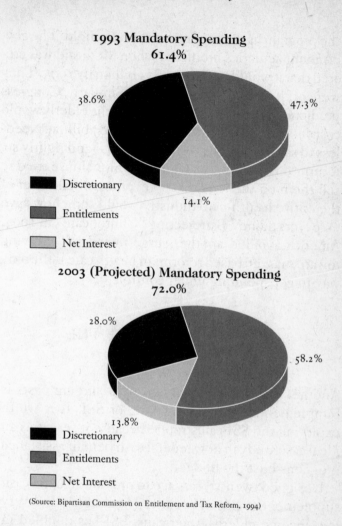

1993 Mandatory Spending 61.4%

38.6%

47.3%

14.1%

◼ Discretionary

◼ Entitlements

◻ Net Interest

2003 (Projected) Mandatory Spending 72.0%

28.0%

58.2%

13.8%

◼ Discretionary

◼ Entitlements

◻ Net Interest

(Source: Bipartisan Commission on Entitlement and Tax Reform, 1994)

By 2003 the share will rise to over 70 percent. The commission termed these numbers "unsettling." We agree.

Government-run health-care programs have been a particular budget-buster. Consider Medicaid, which provides health care for the poor. In just thirty years the program has expanded by a hundredfold. The government actuaries predicted when Medicaid was created that it would cost about $25 billion by 1995. They were off by a factor of nearly ten! Similarly, Congress predicted that by 1990, Medicare for the elderly would cost only $12 billion. Instead it cost $107 billion. Needless to say, Americans were skeptical—and rightly so, it turns out—when the Clinton White House tried to sell them on the idea that a government takeover of the entire health-care industry would somehow save taxpayers money. By rejecting "Clintoncare" in 1994, America avoided another surge in red ink. Moving toward market-based reforms of health care is the only way to get spending under control.

THE BLACK HOLE OF THE WELFARE STATE

Another entitlement program with surging costs is Supplemental Security Income, or SSI. It is worth exploring the SSI catastrophe because it serves as an ideal case study in how federal cash benefit assistance programs bust the budget.

Designed twenty years ago to provide an extra cash supplement to Social Security for disabled and very low–income elderly Americans, SSI has doubled in size in just the past six years. In 1988 there were 4.1 million SSI recipients and federal payments totalled $8.8 billion. In 1993 the program had grown to nearly 6 million recipients receiving federal payments of $20 billion.

What's going on here? Why is this program expanding so uncontrollably? Here's the primary explanation—and the one that is causing widespread taxpayer fury: SSI is now paying out billions of dollars to drug addicts, alcoholics, and immigrants. In just a few short years the SSI program has been converted into an enormous taxpayer ripoff. A 1995 Cato Institute report, for example, cited the following newspaper story in the *Bakersfield Californian* of February 28, 1992: "Linda Torrez said she was paid $8,585.82 by taxpayers for being a junkie. Torrez was arrested last week on charges of possession and use of heroin. During the raid, Bakersfield police found a paper sack with more than $5,000 in it. . . . [Torrez] produced documentation showing the money was hers via a lump sum payment from . . . Supplemental Security Income. She said she is disabled and due to start receiving monthly benefits. Her disability: She is a heroin addict. . . . Addicts or alcoholics must . . . present the Social Security Administration with a . . . payee who is responsible for the benefits. Torrez told police her monitor was Samuel Mendez . . . Mendez was arrested the same day as Torrez, also on charges of heroin use and possession."

Is this incident atypical of how the SSI program spends your tax dollars? Regrettably, no. Today nearly a quarter of a million alcoholics and drug users are collecting SSI "disability" checks. Studies have shown that as many as 90 percent of these substance abusers use their benefits to purchase illegal drugs and alcohol. It is a tragic commentary on the complete failure of SSI's drug addict and alcoholic program that the most common way addicts leave the program is by dying.

Fortunately, some of the welfare reforms we enacted earlier this year will rid the SSI program of some of the most scandalous abuses. But clearly, we have to start investigating our entitlement funding network to root out waste and outright fraud. When it comes to many open-ended entitlement programs like Medicaid and SSI, the federal government has lost control of the reins on spending. And taxpayers are the ones getting trampled.

ENTITLEMENTS AND AMERICA'S FISCAL FUTURE

The real economic danger signal is not how much entitlements have grown in the past, but how much they're expected to expand in the future. Much of this growth is driven by the law of demographics: America's baby boom generation is aging. Soon millions more citizens will be leaving the workforce and entering their retirement years. This means they will start to collect Social Security and Medicare—the two most expensive entitlements.

Here are some of the more frightening official government forecasts for these and other programs, assuming we simply stay the course:

- Over the next fifteen years, Medicare and Medicaid costs will double as a share of national output. Over the next thirty years, these program costs will triple, consuming 10 percent of all the output in the United States economy.

- By 1998 Medicare will start to cost more than it brings in under the dedicated payroll tax. By 2002 the Medicare hospital trust fund will be bankrupt entirely and the future of the program will be in peril.

- Social Security will face a cash deficit in 2013. By 2029 the Social Security system will be insolvent, because the surplus will have been depleted and the annual payroll taxes will not pay for the promised benefits. (Perhaps it shouldn't be too surprising that public opinion polls reveal that more eighteen-year-olds believe in UFOs than that they will ever collect Social Security.)

- By 2030 federal government spending on just four programs—Medicare, Medicaid, Social Security, and federal retirement—will cost as much as Uncle Sam's entire tax revenue collections.

- To keep Medicare and Social Security solvent after 2030, the payroll tax would have to be raised from today's 15 percent rate to 25 percent.

Here is perhaps the most worrisome trend of all. In just seventeen years—that is, by 2012—federal mandatory spending (entitlements plus interest on the debt) will exceed the total amount of revenues collected each year by the U.S. government. Not a penny will be left for roads, bridges, Head Start, the federal courts, drug enforcement, national defense, the FBI, and all the rest. All federal tax dollars will simply be diverted to the purpose of redistributing money from one group to another.

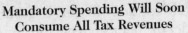

Mandatory Spending Will Soon Consume All Tax Revenues

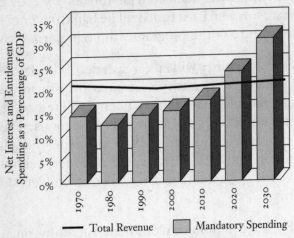

(Source: Bipartisan Commission on Entitlement and Tax Reform, 1994)

We intend to start finding ways to restrain spending on these programs, because we think Americans are entitled to a balanced budget.

THE CLINTON NON-SOLUTION

Hasn't the Clinton budget plan helped avert this budget crisis? Didn't we put government on a diet back in 1993? Unfortunately, no. Contrary to the rhetoric from Washington of tight budget caps and fiscal restraint, federal spending has accelerated rapidly in the 1990s. The federal government is one-third larger today in real terms than when Ronald Reagan left the White House. If Congress had succeeded in simply holding

94

domestic spending to the rate of inflation over the past seven years, the budget would have a surplus this year.

Yes, there has been some genuine progress in slowing federal red ink. From a high of $290 billion in the recession year of 1992, the deficit dropped to $255 billion in 1994 and is expected to dip to about $175 billion in 1995. This progress, however, has nothing to do with recent tax hikes or supposed "airtight" spending caps from either the Bush or Clinton budget deals.

The budget deficit is falling for two major reasons unrelated to Clintonomics. First and foremost, Ronald Reagan won the Cold War. Thanks to the fall of communism, the defense budget has decreased by almost $70 billion in real terms since 1987. Meanwhile, inflation-adjusted spending on everything else in the budget has ballooned by $165 billion. Here's a measure of the fiscal ineptitude in Washington from 1989 to 1994. Despite a multibillion-dollar defense drawdown, the deficit has actually risen sharply since Reagan left office. So if you're wondering what happened to your share of the peace dividend, it probably was invested in the Lawrence Welk Museum, helped underwrite the construction of a new government center in Robert Byrd's hometown in West Virginia, or went to a needy honey bee producer.

The second reason the deficit is falling is that the savings-and-loan crisis is over. In 1990 and 1991 the federal government spent about $55 billion each year to close down failed S&Ls. In 1995 the federal government will actually collect money by selling S&L properties. This amounts to about a $60 billion cosmetic swing in the deficit. Worse yet, because these S&L receipts are scored in the budget not as revenues, but rather as "negative outlays," the "restraint" on federal spending that the White House has been trumpeting is in part an artifact of the budgetary treatment of the S&L sales.

But what is most important is President Clinton's vision for the future. The Clinton budget allows for a gigantic federal domestic spending buildup over the next several years. Over the next seven years the federal budget will *increase* by $600 billion—or almost $6,000 more for every household. The $600 billion increase in spending over the next seven years is the equivalent of pasting on to today's expenditures the entire federal budget from 1980. This is not fiscal restraint. This is business as usual.

PUTTING GOVERNMENT TO THE TEST

Our deficit reduction strategy emphasizes spending cuts and rejects tax increases. In devising our budget plan, we asked ourselves and our constituents four basic questions about the condition of our current government:

• Is the government in Washington too big and does it cost too much?

• Can your family spend money more wisely than Washington can?

• Do you get your money's worth—$15,000 a year—from the federal government?

• Is it fair for the federal government to take one-quarter of your income each year?

Most of our constituents responded with a resounding "yes" to the first two questions and groaned "no" to the last two. Public opinion polls, of course, confirm what we have found from talking to our constituents. For example, Americans were recently asked whether they would favor "smaller government with fewer services," or "larger government with many services." Sixty-three percent said they wanted smaller government, while 27 percent said they wanted larger government.

THE FUTILITY OF RAISING TAXES

We often hear skeptics of our budget approach ask: won't taxes have to be raised to balance the budget? The answer is, no, they shouldn't be raised and they don't have to be raised.

Tax increases have not helped to bring us closer to a balanced budget in recent years. Consider the ill-fated 1990 and 1993 tax increases. Federal revenue growth over the past five years, even after two of the largest tax increases in American history, in 1990 and again in 1993, has been no higher than was expected in 1989 without tax hikes. In fact, federal revenues have been climbing at a slower pace in the 1990s with two tax increases than in the 1980s following Reagan's income tax cut.

Moreover, tax increases invariably invite more wasteful congressional spending. To paraphrase humorist P. J. O'Rourke, giving Washington more money to spend is like giving an eighteen-year-old the car keys and a bottle of whiskey. The historical evidence confirms that tax increases do not lead to deficit reduction. In fact, it may be worse than that. Two years ago researchers at the Joint Economic Committee of Congress made the remarkable finding that every dollar of new taxes over the past forty years has led to $1.59 of additional spending. In other words, whenever Congress has raised taxes, the deficit has gone up, not down. Nobel Prize–winning economist Milton Friedman explains this strange occurrence this way: "Government spends whatever the tax system will raise plus the largest level of deficits that the nation will tolerate." President Reagan stated this rule in a slightly different way: never give a big spender a bigger allowance.

But even if we were to suspend our disbelief for a moment and assume that tax increases could be devoted entirely to deficit reduction, we don't think taxpayers would be enthusiastic about this solution. The Institute for Policy Innovation, located in Lewisville, Texas, discovered that if Congress were to try to balance the budget by raising taxes, this would require the average family's tax liability to about double over the course of the next twenty-five years. On average, by 2020, the average American worker would pay $27,500 (in

1990 dollars) in federal taxes alone. More than 40 percent of a worker's paycheck would be seized by the federal taxman that year. With state and local taxes, the government's take could rise to 55 percent of middle-income worker paychecks by the third decade of the twenty-first century.

OUR CHALLENGE, OUR COMMITMENT

Now, for the best-kept secret in Washington: to balance the budget by 2002, we don't have to "cut" federal spending at all. Recall that federal outlays are expected to climb by roughly $600 billion by 2002. If we can just slow this spending increase to $200 billion, we will have met our commitment to balance the budget. The two graphs on the next page tell the whole story. Under the Clinton path, spending increases from $1.6 trillion in 1996 to $2.2 trillion by 2002. Under the House Republican plan, spending increases "only" to $1.8 trillion. In other words, we will increase spending, just not as much.

Our challenge is to spend "just" $12 trillion over the next seven years, rather than the $13 trillion the Democrats wish to spend. Even our plan is hardly austere: it would still be the largest seven-year total of spending in peacetime history, even after adjusting for inflation. The case we will take to the American public throughout 1995 is straightforward: *Shouldn't government in Washington be able to do everything it is supposed to do over the next seven years with $12 trillion?*

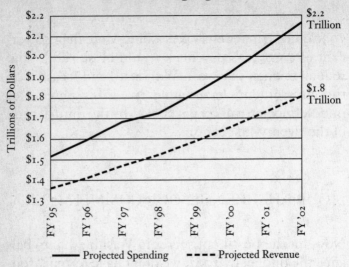

The Continuing Nightmare

Trillions of Dollars

$2.2 $2.2 Trillion

$1.8 Trillion

FY '95   FY '96   FY '97   FY '98   FY '99   FY '00   FY '01   FY '02

—— Projected Spending   ---- Projected Revenue

(Source: Congressional Budget Office, 1995)

The Path to a Balanced Budget

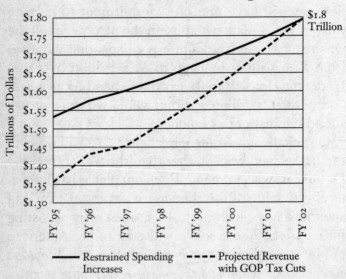

Trillions of Dollars

$1.8 Trillion

FY '95   FY '96   FY '97   FY '98   FY '99   FY '00   FY '01   FY '02

—— Restrained Spending   ---- Projected Revenue
Increases   with GOP Tax Cuts

(Source: Congressional Budget Office, 1995)

A NEW BUDGET ACT

Part of the challenge of eliminating the deficit involves reforming the way we put our budget together. Why is this important? The last time Congress overhauled its budget rules and procedures was 1974—and we haven't balanced the budget since then! As part of our commitment to balancing the budget, we will call for a new budget act that will contain many of the following reforms, some of which were adopted in *Contract with America*:

- *Line item veto authority for the President.* The President should have the power to cut out the waste that Congress won't.

- *Ending baseline budgeting so that Congress can't continue to call a $600 billion spending increase a "cut."* No more false and misleading advertising in the budget. We will now use 1995's actual spending total as the baseline for the next year's budget. If we spend more than the current year, this is an increase; if we spend less, it is a cut.

- *Airtight spending caps for domestic and defense spending.* These caps will ensure that Congress does not try to balance the budget with tax increases. They will also prevent Congress from raiding the defense budget to pay for more social programs.

- *A supermajority vote to raise any taxes.* The *Contract* requires a 60 percent vote to raise income taxes. This was a good start. But now we believe that this hurdle should eventually apply to *all* revenue raising bills. It is a testament to Washington's skewed sense of priorities that Congress now imposes a supermajority requirement rule to *cut* taxes, but requires a simple majority to raise them. It's easier for Congress to take your money than to return it. Americans have been hit with twelve tax hikes in the past twenty years: each one has succeeded in further expanding the size of government, rather than reducing the debt. No more.

- *A statute of limitation on all spending programs.* It has been said that the closest thing to immortality on this earth is a federal government program. Congress doesn't know how to end programs—even years and years after their missions have been accomplished. Our sunset provision will require the true "reinvention" of programs by forcing the reexamination of every program including entitlements, every five years.

- *Debt buy-down provision.* This empowers taxpayers to dedicate up to 10 percent of their income tax payments to retirement of the national debt. Politicians earmark spending all the time. Why can't taxpayers?

- *A legislative balanced budget requirement.* We will set into law a deficit reduction path that brings us to a balanced budget by 2002—and then keeps the budget balanced (except during time of war) forever thereafter. To protect against Congress shirking its deficit reduction responsibility, we will establish an across-the-board spending reduction mechanism, applying to all programs except Social Security, to ensure compliance.

- *Dynamic scoring of tax policy changes.* Congress unfailingly overestimates the revenue collections from tax increases and underestimates the revenue losses from tax cuts. This is because the budget scorekeepers fail to take account of the economy-wide response to changes in tax policy. Dynamic scoring will yield more accurate tax revenue estimates, and thus encourage better policy.

- *Porkbusters legislation.* To end wasteful, pork-barrel spending, we will establish several criteria to reject spending projects that do not have national importance. This anti-waste legislation has been promoted for many years by Rep. Harris Fawell of Illinois.

VICTORY OVER GOVERNMENT

To regain control of our nation's economic destiny, we need to regain control of our government's finances. Our federal government is supposed to be of, by, and for the people—not of, by, and for the special-interest lobbyists in Washington. The Joint Economic Committee of Congress has devised a yearly index of how much government costs American workers. The index is called "Victory Over Government Day" because it marks the day in the year that Americans stop working for government—to cover the cost of its taxes and borrowing—and start working for themselves. The

Cost of Government Day in 1995 falls on June 4, almost halfway through the calendar. If our *Contract with America* provisions are enacted into law as well as the GOP fiscal plan to balance the budget by 2002, then the Victory Over Government Day will retreat to May 26. In other words, by balancing the budget and enacting the *Contract with America* every American worker will receive the equivalent of a two-week bonus. And that's something you can take to the bank.

5
Balancing the Budget

Isn't it about time we put Uncle Sam on a diet? Hillary Clinton and former U.S. Surgeon General C. Everett Koop held a Rose Garden press conference in 1994 to announce that Americans are too fat. They said Americans should trim down because obesity costs $8 billion a year in lost output and poor health. How ironic to hear the Washington Establishment tell the American people that *they* are too fat and out-of-shape. The truth is that today's federal government has become bloated, inefficient, bureaucratic, and out of touch with the concerns of ordinary Americans. It spends too much time doing things it shouldn't do, and too little time doing the things it should.

Our first priority in transforming the federal government is to tirelessly search through the cavernous agencies of government for wasteful and unnecessary spending and then surgically extract it from the budget. One reason government is so expensive is that Washington spends about twice as much on overhead and administration costs as private businesses do.

But we have to confess from the start: balancing the budget won't be easy and it won't be fun. For reasons discussed in the previous chapter, to eliminate federal red ink, we also need to reform many of the most politically sensitive programs—particularly the fast-growing entitlements. Our general approach to entitlement reforms will be to expand choice and rely on market solutions.

Some of the steps we will take to achieve the goal of a balanced budget won't always be popular. Any politician would prefer to "cut" checks rather than cut spending. But for too many years Congress has been run by check writers. It is precisely that irresponsible behavior that created our deficit-spending crisis in the first place. As Speaker Newt Gingrich said to the American public in his nationally televised speech in April 1995: "The congressional voting card has become the most expensive credit card in the world."

As we undertake our mission to balance the budget, we will surely make mistakes. But, unlike what you've received under forty years of a Democratic-controlled Congress, we promise this from the outset: *no more budget gimmickry, no more blue smoke and mirrors, and no more cowardice in the face of special-interest pleadings. We will make the tough and, yes, sometimes unpopular choices.*

We hope to do this in partnership with our Democratic colleagues in Congress. Many of them voted with us on the *Contract with America*; and we're confident these and others will join our balanced budget crusade. We hope to do it in partnership with President Clinton—although frankly we are none too confident of helpful White House participation. We view the Clinton budget as a profound disappointment—an unwillingness to provide the leadership this crisis deserves. Indeed, we view the "don't worry, be happy" attitude that underlies the Clinton budget as a padlock on progress. So, although we would welcome the President's leadership on the budget issue, since very little appears to be forthcoming, we may have no option but to take the lead ourselves.

Most important, we hope to balance the budget in partnership with the American people. Over the past several months we have been listening to and learning from America—and we'll continue to do so—to find out your ideas on how to make government more cost-effective. We need help from America's taxpayers because we have to acknowledge from the start that we don't have all the answers as to how to cure Washington of this cancerous deficit.

BUDGET BALANCING PRINCIPLES

To balance the budget by the year 2002, we have to find a way to trim roughly $1.2 trillion out of a $13 trillion of planned federal outlays over the next seven years. We will repeat what was said before: *Spending does not have to go down in any single year to balance the budget. It just has to go up more slowly than planned.* In 1996 the federal government will spend $1.6 trillion. In 2002 the federal treasury will collect $1.8 trillion in tax revenues. Our task is to make sure that spending "only" goes up by $200 billion ($2,000 *more* for every American household) over the next seven years. Remember this when the special-interest groups start lambasting our "cuts" as painful and unfair.

The graph below starkly reveals our two choices. The solid line is the President's proposed budget deficit path; the broken line is our balanced budget plan. Under Clinton's plan, the deficit in 2002 will be more than $300 billion. In our plan, the deficit will be entirely eliminated.

To accomplish our mission, we have developed the following fifteen budget-balancing principles:

1. Promote tax and regulatory policies that encourage economic growth and thereby help reduce the deficit painlessly. If we can increase the annual economic growth rate by just one percentage point over the next seven years, almost half of the budget deficit will disappear.

The Two Choices Before America

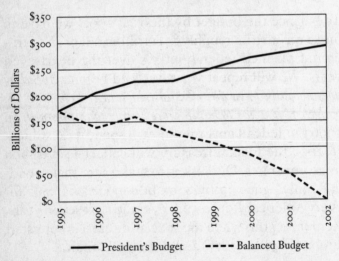

(Source: House Budget Committee, 1995)

2. Cut Congress's own budget first.
3. Carve out the pervasive duplication, waste, and pork-barrel spending in the budget.
4. Replace the welfare state with an opportunity society.
5. Move money and power out of Washington—back to families, communities, and states.
6. Privatize services and assets that are more properly provided by private businesses and charities, neighborhood groups, and nonprofit institutions.
7. Reduce our foreign aid expenditures substantially.
8. Consolidate and eliminate entirely several Cabinet agencies.
9. Accept the sound budget-cutting ideas in President Clinton's own budgets.
10. Cut welfare to corporate America.
11. Eliminate nearly 300 programs that no longer serve a useful function—and many others that never did.
12. Demand value for our defense dollars while promoting strong national security.
13. Protect, preserve, and improve Medicare.
14. Seek a national commitment of all Americans to be part of the budget-balancing solution.

Here's how we plan to go about each of these objectives.

CUT CONGRESS FIRST

If we're going to demand cuts in government pro-grams, shouldn't we cut our own budget as well? Congress is now the most expensive legislature in the world. In 1994 the budget for the Congress was roughly $2.8 billion. This was an 800 percent rise since 1965 and a 4,000 percent rise since 1946. To put these num-bers in perspective, the legislature's spending on itself has grown at six times the rate of inflation since the end of the Second World War and three times faster than the defense budget.

Of course, one of our first actions in the *Contract with America* was to reduce committee staffing by one-third and abolish three subcommittees. But we're not through trimming the fat in spending on ourselves. We will continue to cut staffing levels, sell at least one congressional office building, privatize one parking lot, and systematically review every function in the legislative branch for cost savings. This will symbol-ize our commitment to creating a leaner, more cost-efficient federal government.

END PORK-BARREL SPENDING

Washington, D.C., is a city where thick carvings of pork are served every year during budget season. Pork-barrel spending is taxpayer money that is targeted to specific congressional districts, but serves no overrid-ing national purpose. One of the more irresponsible examples of a local program that received federal funding was construction dollars for the Lansing, Michigan, airport. A sign outside the entrance of the new airport when it was opened said it all: BUILT WITHOUT TAXES FROM LANSING, MI. Why not? Isn't it mostly the people who live in Lansing who use the airport? Wouldn't it make more sense for the citizens of Lansing to pay for the airport rather than people who live in Fresno, California, or Burlington, Vermont? What that sign might just well have said was: BUILT BY THE SUCKERS WHO SEND THEIR MONEY TO WASHINGTON.

There are hundreds of other similar incidents of Congress spending scarce tax dollars on projects of purely local significance. Here are just a few examples from 1994's budget of your tax dollars hard at work these days:

- $2 million for a farmer's market in Toledo.

- $750,000 for a SciTrek museum in downtown Atlanta.

- $600,000 for fish farming research in Stuttgart, Arkansas.

- $1.5 million for a survey of Amtrak riders between New York and Boston.

- $13 million for the Robert C. Byrd Locks and Dam in West Virginia.

- $1.2 million for a neighborhood advisory commission in Washington, D.C.

- $1.3 million for the D.C. Taxicab Commission (this is a city that is nearly bankrupt, mind you).

- $3.4 million for Textile Clothing Tech. Corp.

- $7 million for the Luis Muñoz Marin Airport in Puerto Rico.

- $1 million for buses in Santa Barbara—one of the wealthiest towns in America.

The list could go on for pages and pages. But you get the picture. And it's not just small change. The 1991 highway bill, for example, contained $5 billion of "road demonstration projects" including a Chicago parking garage and an exit ramp to an amusement park in Toledo, Ohio.

We will target this kind of parochial spending for the cutting board. And we have to confess that this kind of parochial spending is *a bipartisan bad habit*—almost *all* of us in Congress strive to bring the "free" dollars from Washington home to our districts. But the game has to end. With the "Pork-busters Bill" described in the last chapter and the line-item veto we enacted in 1995, much of this pork can be sliced from the budget.

END TAXPAYER RIP-OFFS

Everyone remembers the famous incidents in the early 1980s where the Pentagon was found spending $600 on toilet seats, $300 on hammers, $14 on a nail. These kinds of abuses of taxpayer dollars continue—and are probably worse today. The Farmers Home Administration is a case in point. Since its inception in 1935 the agency has loaned over $170 billion to farmers and rural communities. Today some $56 billion of this principal remains unpaid. In fact, the Heritage Foundation reports that "now the FmHA is making new loans to individuals so they can repay old loans." Despite this record of delinquency and failure, the program has never been thoroughly reformed and Uncle Sam still spends $2.6 billion a year making new loans.

The wool and mohair subsidy program at the USDA is supposed to help small sheep herders. Earlier this year *The Wall Street Journal* reported that the third largest recipient of wool and mohair subsidies in Lincoln County, New Mexico, is none other than ABC's Sam Donaldson. Each year $97,000 in subsidy checks are delivered to his house in suburban Virginia. The *Journal* reports that millions of dollars of farm price support checks are delivered to "farmers" who live in cities.

The sugar price support program is mostly aid to the rich. An estimated 40 percent of the $1.4 billion sugar price support program benefits the largest 1 percent of sugar farms. The thirty-three largest sugar cane plantations each receive more than $1 million.

A congressional investigative team discovered in 1994 that federal environmental cleanup and defense contractors had been milking federal taxpayers for millions of dollars in entertainment, recreation, and party expenses. Ecology and Environment, Inc., of Lancaster, New York, spent $243,000 of funds designated for environmental cleanup on "employee morale" and $37,000 on tennis lessons, bike races, golf tournaments, and other entertainment.

All examples of your tax dollars at work—or, rather, at play.

One of the options that we are investigating to exterminate these taxpayer rip-offs is the creation of another Waste Commission, modeled after the 1982 Grace Commission. Its purpose would be to identify where we could save money by ending these kinds of abuses. Sen. Connie Mack has proposed that such a commission could be modeled after the Dick Armey base closings commission, whereby the Congress would have to vote up or down on the entire list of budget savings. We think such an approach could yield tens of billions of dollars in savings.

PRIVATIZE FEDERAL ASSETS AND SERVICES

All over the world state-owned assets and enterprises are being privatized at a frenzied pace. The California-based Reason Foundation calculates that from 1985 through 1992, $330 billion worth of public assets and enterprises were privatized around the world.

• Since 1980 China has gone from nearly 80 percent state ownership to less than 50 percent.

• The Thatcher revolution in Britain led to the sale of nearly $100 billion of publicly run businesses, including British Telecom, British Airways, and Jaguar.

• Fast-growing Chile has privatized 75 percent of its state-owned enterprises over the past twenty years.

The United States is the laggard on the privatization front. Very little has been turned over to the private sector. Even during the Reagan years, when privatization became a central theme in Washington, there was much rhetoric but little action. In 1988 the bipartisan presidential Commission on Privatization issued a report entitled *Privatization: Toward More Effective Government.* The commission identified dozens of government activities that should be turned over to the private sector, including public housing, federal loan programs, and Amtrak. It concluded that public ownership and management of assets and industries is costly to the American economy. Often the assets are misused, underused, or simply lay idle—as is the case with so much of our federally owned land. The Postal Service monopoly, for example, is estimated to constitute at least a $5 billion per year drain on the economy.

For the first time ever in Congress, we want to comprehensively review activities that might be better managed and operated privately. Some of the federal activities that might be considered for privatization include:

- Nonenvironmentally sensitive federal lands

- Federal oil reserves, valued at $400 billion

- Certain Amtrak routes

- The National Endowment for the Arts and the National Endowment for the Humanities

- The Corporation for Public Broadcasting

- The $250 billion federal loan portfolio

- The Federal Helium Reserve

- Public housing units, which could be transferred to the tenants

- Federal dams

- The Naval Petroleum Reserve

- The Air Traffic Control System.

Here's one example of how privatization can save money and improve people's lives. For the past thirty years, the federal government has constructed hugely expensive public housing projects for the poor. These units have become unlivable traps, havens for gangs, poverty, drugs, and despair. *The Washington Post* recently described public housing projects as "one of the nation's most enduring symbols of government failure."

Why not correct this multibillion-dollar failure by transferring the ownership of the units to the residents themselves? In some cases the units could be sold to the tenants; in others, we would give them away and get the government away from managing them. Experience suggests that private management and tenant ownership can make all the difference in the world. For example, at Washington, D.C.'s Kenilworth-Parkside project, the transition to private ownership has given the residents a greater stake in the condition of their new homes, their neighborhoods, and their own lives. Everyone has come out a winner: the taxpayers, the residents, and the surrounding communities.

Another program where privatization might be appropriate is Amtrak. When Amtrak first came under government ownership in 1971 during the Nixon administration, Congress called the takeover a "noble experiment" to make the money-losing passenger rail service profitable again. Yet, twenty-five years later the trains still lose $1 billion a year—with no end of subsidies in sight. Today Amtrak is by far America's most highly subsidized form of intercity transportation with an average taxpayer cost of some $25 for every passenger who climbs aboard. In the 1980s some western lines were so expensive to operate that it would have been cheaper for the government to close them down and buy each passenger a plane ticket paid for by the taxpayer. Federal subsidies to Amtrak are ten to twenty times higher than those offered to intercity bus and air travelers.

On Amtrak's silver anniversary it is timely and appropriate to ask what lies around the curve for the railroad. It may be time for Congress to honor the pledge made to taxpayers back in 1971 and map out a strategy and firm timetable for returning Amtrak to the private sector. This could be accomplished by phasing out Amtrak subsidies over no more than five years and then giving the operations of the railroad to its current workers, management, or other private investors.

The 1988 bipartisan commission projected that privatization in these and many other areas could save tens of billions of taxpayer dollars. We think that private ownership of many of these activities would actually lead to improved service and better management, thus benefiting both taxpayers and service recipients.

CUT FOREIGN AID

The federal government spends $22 billion a year on international affairs. Some of these funds go to carrying out the legitimate foreign-affairs activities of the State Department. But most of the expenditures are for bilateral and multilateral foreign aid to other nations. These programs include U.S. contributions to the United Nations, the World Bank, and the International Monetary Fund (IMF). After tens of billions of dollars of U.S. taxpayer funding of these programs, there is not a scintilla of evidence that these programs have had any positive effect in promoting economic development.

Cato Institute scholars Doug Bandow and Ian Vasquez argue persuasively in their book *Perpetuating Poverty* that America's foreign aid programs do real harm to developing countries. For example, misguided IMF policy advice led up to the peso devaluation in Mexico. In other developing nations the IMF and World Bank have urged policymakers to raise taxes to close budget deficits—which is exactly the wrong fiscal prescription. Fred Smith, the president of the Competitive Enterprise Institute, summarized the worthlessness of these programs in one sentence: "Foreign aid taxes poor people in rich countries and gives the money to rich people in poor countries."

The American public wants foreign aid cut because they think it's a vast waste of money. All of the evidence indicates that they are right. We should be exporting our products and our democratic institutions to these nations, not our tax dollars.

CONSOLIDATE THE CABINET

The first Congress created just three Cabinet agencies: the State Department, the Department of War, and the Treasury Department. Remarkable as it may seem today, for about the first fifty years of our nation, one single agency, the Treasury Department, handled all domestic affairs—everything. In 1849 the Interior Department was founded, and many civilian activities, such as road building, were transferred to the purview of this agency.

The federal government rapidly spawned new domestic Cabinet agencies over the next hundred years. The Justice Department was created in 1870, followed by the Agriculture Department in 1889, followed by the Commerce Department in 1903, which was followed by the Labor Department in 1913.

Since the Second World War a torrent of new agencies was created. Included were: Health, Education, and Welfare in 1953; Housing and Urban Development in 1965; Transportation in 1966; the Energy Department in 1977; the Education Department in 1979; and the Veterans Affairs Department in 1989.

The Agriculture Department is a case study in how agencies grow and grow. Originally the purpose of the USDA was to collect agriculture statistics for the government. To do so, it received a $1,000 appropriation. By the mid-1930s, after President Franklin Roosevelt began to fund direct farm subsidies, the USDA budget grew to $250 million. Even back then the *Chicago Tribune* commented that the Agriculture Department had become "lost in its own weeds."

Sixty years later the weeds have reached eye level. The USDA budget eclipsed $30 billion in the mid-1980s and today it continues to spend tax dollars subsidizing many prosperous farmers. USDA field offices now provide taxpayer-funded courses in urban gardening, sewing, and gourmet cooking. Agencies never die; they just find new missions.

We want to completely rethink the federal farm subsidies issue and eventually reduce the USDA mission. We hear more and more from our own farmers—especially small farmers—that the USDA's programs are outdated and an increasing liability rather than an asset to their bottom line. We think many farmers would gladly trade a cut in crop subsidies for a cut in federal regulations and red tape.

A group of thirty House Republican freshmen led by Rep. Sam Brownback of Kansas wants to close down no fewer than four Cabinet agencies. While there is still no consensus on all of these consolidation ideas, here are some of the more ambitious proposals from some House Republicans:

- *Merge the departments of Education and Labor to save $4 billion.* Milwaukee Mayor John Norquist, a Democrat, says, "The U.S. Department of Education adds no value to America's inner-city schools." Since it was created, test scores and virtually every other objective measure of school performance have declined.

- *Eliminate the Commerce Department to save $7.7 billion over five years.* The General Accounting Office says that "the Department of Commerce shares its mission with at least seventy-one federal departments, agencies, and offices."

- *Eliminate the Energy Department to save $20 billion over five years.* The Energy Department was born during the Jimmy Carter presidency at the height of the 1970s energy crisis. Almost all of its prescriptions then to deal with the crisis succeeded in making it worse. Its price controls and windfall profits tax prolonged the crisis by driving U.S. producers out of the market. It spent $2 billion on the synthetic fuels corporation, which it thought would be the next great alternative energy source. The project flopped and never produced a single kilowatt of electricity. Its supporters want to retain the agency so as to develop a "national energy strategy." We already have a national energy strategy that works very well: it's called the free market.

• *Shut down HUD.* HUD now has a vast bureaucracy of 13,000 workers—most of whom work behind desks in Washington—and many have never even been to declining cities like Detroit and Gary, Indiana. Mayor Bret Schundler of Jersey City, New Jersey, complains that "the major beneficiaries of HUD are not the inner-city poor, they are federal workers, urban lobbyists, government contractors, mortgage bankers, and the construction industry." Since the mid-1960s when many of HUD's Great Society programs were created, the major industrial cities of America have lost 4 million people—and about as many jobs. Whatever it is that HUD is doing to help our struggling cities—it is not working.

We have not decided exactly which of these agencies will be reorganized and which will be closed. But for the first time ever, we will consolidate the Cabinet agency structure. Our great corporations are under pressure every day to perform, cut costs, be efficient. For too long the big agencies of government have just sat there, immovable, like comatose dinosaurs.

ACCEPT CLINTON'S BUDGET CUTS

As a sign of good faith that we want to work in a bipartisan fashion with the White House, we will incorpo-

rate many of the President's own budget-cutting proposals from the past three years into our fiscal plan.
We like many of the ideas in the Clinton blueprint—
we just wish there were more of them. Vice President
Al Gore has some helpful suggestions in his *Reinventing Government* report as well. Here are some of the
Clinton proposed program cutbacks and terminations
we wholeheartedly agree with:

- Wastewater treatment grants

- Nuclear reactor research and development

- HUD special-purpose grants

- Small Business Administration grants and loans

- Uranium-enrichment programs

- Selected student loan programs

- The Agency for International Development

- International security assistance

- The Appalachian Regional Commission

Wherever there is a bipartisan consensus that certain federal programs don't work, it is our pledge to
move quickly to eliminate them.

ATTACK CORPORATE WELFARE

Isn't it time we pushed corporate America off the federal dole? Corporate subsidies and handouts have become pervasive in the federal budget. Private research estimates place the annual price tag for federal handouts to corporate America at as much as $80 billion. Within some Cabinet agencies, such as the U.S. departments of Agriculture and Commerce, almost every spending program underwrites private business activities. The following is a list of some of the more expensive taxpayer subsidies to industries and firms:

- Over the past twenty years the Forest Service has spent more than $3 billion to build 340,000 miles of roads—more than eight times the length of the interstate highway system—primarily for the benefit of private logging companies.

- The U.S. Department of Agriculture Market Promotion Program spends $110 million per year underwriting the cost of advertising American products abroad. In 1991 American taxpayers spent $2.9 million advertising Pillsbury muffins and pies, $465,000 advertising McDonald's Chicken McNuggets, and $1.2 million boosting the international sales of American Legend mink coats.

- The Clinton administration wants to spend $490 million in 1995 for the Advanced Technology Program

(ATP), a government lottery reserved for high-tech companies.

- The half-billion-dollar-a-year Technology Reinvestment Project, another Clinton administration brainchild run from the Pentagon, hands out checks to *Fortune* 500 companies for developing "civilian technologies." In other words, it pays these companies millions of dollars to do what 98 percent of America's businesses do at no cost to the taxpayer. In 1994 award recipients included such *Fortune* 500 companies as Texas Instruments ($13 million), 3M ($6 million), Chrysler Corporation ($6 million), Hewlett-Packard ($10 million), and Rockwell ($7 million).

Why do we need any of this aid to dependent corporations? Although the program's supporters maintain that these tax dollars promote the competitiveness of U.S. industry, this argument is unpersuasive. Years of historical experience prove that government agencies have a much less successful track record than do private capital markets at correctly selecting winners. The average delinquency rate is almost three times higher for government loan programs (8 percent) than for commercial lenders (3 percent).

Make no mistake about it: we want the United States to have the most competitive and profitable industries in the world. We just reject the idea that the best way for government to help business in America is one business at a time. The most important steps that we in Congress can take to truly increase the profitability and job creation potential of U.S. industry is to cut taxes, such as on capital gains, and eliminate the budget deficit.

So, House Republicans not only plan to end welfare as we know it. We intend to end corporate welfare as we know it as well.

TERMINATE UNNECESSARY FEDERAL PROGRAMS

After decades of inventing hundreds upon hundreds of new programs, we in Congress now need to prove that we can actually get rid of things that are obsolete, inefficient, or counterproductive. If we cannot, government will be forever paralyzed from adapting and responding to the challenges of the next century. We won't be able to wisely and judiciously spend money on important investments for the future, because we will be stuck with an arsenal of programs fighting yesterday's problems. We will suffer perpetually from the tyranny of the status quo. That is the essence of bad government.

To break through the fiscal gridlock, our budget proposal recommends eliminating 283 obsolete programs, 14 agencies, and 68 commissions. Of course, pulling the funding plug on unnecessary programs will be a novel experience for federal lawmakers. As we have noted, the closest thing to immortality is a federal program. Since 1980 only a small handful of the thousands of agencies in the budget have been closed down, despite a growing bipartisan consensus that tens of billions of dollars in savings could be generated by such measures. Here are just a few examples of programs that need to be cut or eliminated:

- *The Economic Development Administration (EDA)*

The EDA was created in the 1960s to help revitalize economically distressed urban and rural areas. The program evidently has an expansive concept of "distressed." More than 80 percent of the U.S. population lives in areas that have received an EDA grant. In 1988 a review of EDA grants found that fifteen of the thirty-five communities with the lowest unemployment rates in the nation received EDA money. Asheville, North Carolina, had an unemployment rate of 2.3 percent that year but received a $55,000 EDA grant. Poughkeepsie, New York, has a 2.4 percent unemployment rate, less than half the national average, but received a $50,000 payment.

In 1987 Fort Worth, Texas, received a $4.5 million EDA grant to rehabilitate the Fort Worth stockyards. This was an unusually large grant for the EDA, particularly because Fort Worth is not "distressed." How did the project get so much money? Hint: the congressman from Fort Worth at the time was Speaker of the House Jim Wright. This was no mere coincidence. As Murray Weidenbaum, former chairman of the President's Council of Economic Advisers, has noted, the EDA has become the ultimate "urban pork-barrel program."

- *The Appalachian Regional Commission (ARC)*

The ARC was also a Great Society program intended to bring economic development to the poorest areas of rural Appalachia. But what started as a targeted aid concept has become a federal giveaway. As of 1990 there were ninety counties eligible for "distressed county" funding from ARC. Today, thirty years after Lyndon Johnson launched the program, the poverty rate in Appalachia hasn't budged much, despite the $6 billion infusion of federal funds. Perhaps part of the problem is the absurd use of these tax dollars. For example, in 1995 ARC will spend $750,000 to help build a football stadium that will serve as the practice field for the Carolina Panthers National Football League franchise. We love football too, but the NFL is hardly "distressed."

- *Urban transit grants*

The federal government has spent more than $50 billion on transit subsidies since 1965 and yet fewer people use public transit today than when these programs began thirty years ago. Huge white elephants on wheels have been funded, from Metrorail in Miami (or "Metrofail" as south Floridians derisively call the rail system, because so few ride it) to Detroit's People Mover (which *The Detroit News* once called the most absurd transportation project in American history). Shortly before he retired from the Senate, Democrat William Proxmire awarded his celebrated Golden Fleece award to the Federal Transit Administration for "playing Santa Claus to America's cities." Sorry, there's no money left with which to be playing Santa Claus.

• *The Rural Electrification Administration (REA)*

The REA, the federal government's ultimate dinosaur, was created in 1935 to bring electricity and telephone service to rural America, and its mission has been accomplished. More than 98 percent of all rural homes now have access to electrical and phone service. Yet the agency continues to loan money at subsidized rates to rural electric co-ops and has even tried to expand its mission to cable TV hookup.

The major beneficiaries of REA and its sister programs, the federal Power Marketing Administrations (PMAs), are large and profitable electric utility cooperatives. REA and PMA subsidies, roughly $2 billion a year, help hold down the costs of running ski resorts in Aspen, Colorado, five-star hotels in Hilton Head, South Carolina, and gambling casinos in Las Vegas, Nevada.

• *Low Income Home Energy Assistance Program (LIHEAP)*

The federal government spends hundreds of millions of dollars a year promoting energy conservation, while it spends billions of dollars on programs such as REA, the Power Marketing Administrations, and LIHEAP to subsidize the use of more energy. LIHEAP was created to help poor families heat their homes during the Arab oil embargo of the 1970s when energy prices tripled. We now intend to inform the careerists in Washington that the energy crisis ended more than a decade ago. If Congress is genuinely concerned about the costs of energy to low-income families then the solution is to stop taxing oil and gas so heavily.

- *The Small Business Administration (SBA)*

The SBA "assists" less than half of one percent of all small businesses in America. In other words, about 99.7 percent of all small businesses start up without a handout from government. There is little support for these lending programs, even among the small business community. The SBA has had an inglorious track record in selecting businesses to finance. Some of its loan programs have had repayment delinquency rates of over 20 percent. We know how to help generate new small businesses: cut the capital gains tax, lower payroll taxes, end the proliferation of regulations, and eliminate the deficit.

- *The National Endowment for the Arts (NEA)*

The NEA and its sister agency, the National Endowment for the Humanities (NEH), should be privatized. It is our view that arts and culture play a vital role in society, but that there is no rationale for government financing of such activities. Studies show that the clientele for most arts and culture programs are those with high or above average incomes. Americans who benefit from these programs can afford to pay for them. Many NEA projects—such as the Mapplethorpe exhibit—and NEH curricula—with its anti-Western civilization bias—are offensive to Americans. Taxpayers should not be compelled to pay for them.

- *The Corporation for Public Broadcasting (CPB)*

The federal government spends about $300 million a year subsidizing public broadcasting. With the widespread availability of cable TV and the launching of many new educational channels, such as the Discovery Channel and the new History Channel, the original rationale for CPB is gone. We are reasonably certain that National Public Radio and all of public TV's quality children's programming would survive, and probably flourish, without taxpayer financing. Federal contributions to CPB only constitute 14 percent of its budget. In 1994 "Barney," the purple dinosaur, grossed $800 million in sales and "Sesame Street" nearly $1 billion.

- *AmeriCorps*

AmeriCorps is a program launched with lofty intentions by President Clinton to allow young Americans to participate in national service activities. Unfortunately, after eighteen months the program is a scandalous mess. AmeriCorp's "volunteers" are costing taxpayers $7.27 an hour. Nebraska received a $450,000 AmeriCorp grant to recruit twenty-three participants—that's $20,000 per "volunteer" just to get them signed up. When *Rolling Stone* magazine asked one teenager why he was participating, his answer was brutally frank:

"money." John P. Walters of the New Citizenship Project notes that "AmeriCorps is unnecessary and corrupts the true spirit of volunteerism. Overpaid volunteers participating in programs approved and regulated by a federal bureaucracy is a corruption of genuine, healthy charity." We strongly support volunteer programs in our society. But taxpayer-financed volunteerism is a contradiction in terms.

DEMAND VALUE FOR OUR DEFENSE DOLLARS

The single most vital activity of the federal government is to provide for the national defense. We will not allow Democrats' desires for deep defense cuts to leave America with another hollow military. The Republican position in the post–Cold War era is, to borrow a phrase from Texas Sen. Phil Gramm, "When the lion and lamb lay down together, we want to make sure that America is still the lion."

We strongly disapprove of the strategy of President Clinton and previous Congresses to raid the defense budget to pay for more domestic spending. We think the Clinton budget plan goes too far in cutting spending on many vital national security programs. However, in the context of the strategy of achieving a balanced budget, we recognize that all programs—even defense spending—must be trimmed. We've already made a commitment in our *Contract with America* to cut international peacekeeping funds. We want to make sure that additional budget cuts in defense come from the fat and not out of the muscle of our military. We will not salute waste in Washington just because it's wearing a uniform. The Pentagon is hardly a paragon of cost-efficiency.

We know one place to start cutting immediately. In recent years liberals in Congress have taken to hiding domestic spending in our defense budget. In 1994 this included $6 billion of spending on such items as the Goodwill Games, medical research, and business subsidies. In the future all our defense dollars will go toward national security, not pork.

PROTECT, PRESERVE, AND IMPROVE MEDICARE

The Medicare program is protected by a group of six trustees who are required by law to give a yearly accounting of the program's safety and solvency. These trustees include four senior presidential appointees: the secretaries of Treasury, Health and Human Services, and Labor; the commissioner of Social Security; and two members of the public, one Democrat and one Republican.

On April 3, 1995, the Medicare Board of Trustees reported for the second year in a row that the Medicare Trust Fund will be bankrupt in seven years. If, as they predict, the Trust Fund goes bankrupt, then by law the federal government must stop providing for inpatient hospital and other trust fund–paid services. Medicare's collapse would be a catastrophe for the more than 32 million senior citizens and 4 million disabled people who depend on it. That is why one of the most urgent reforms we can make in 1995 is to save Medicare from impending bankruptcy. Leaving Medicare on automatic pilot would mean that the program would soon cease to exist. The graph below shows the fiscal and human tragedy that awaits us if we don't act to save the system.

It is not enough to merely avoid bankruptcy. For our future generations, Medicare must return to a sound footing. We will aim to give an individual turning 65 today the security of knowing they will still have a Medicare program not only seven years from now when they turn seventy-two, but also when they reach eighty-two and ninety-two. We need to make long-term reforms—not just apply a quick fix—because in thirty-five years the number of Americans over seventy will

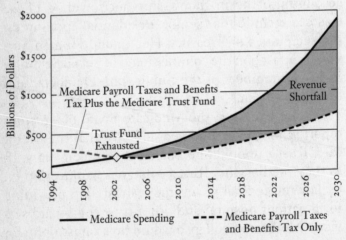

Medicare's Path to Bankruptcy

(Source: Entitlement Commission; Joint Economic Committe, 1994)

have doubled, while the number of U.S. workers supporting each retiree will have dropped from five to three. While our efforts to protect Medicare from bankruptcy and to balance the budget by the year 2002 will take place simultaneously, it is important to remember that even if we had a balanced budget today, we would still have to take action to save the Medicare Trust Fund from bankruptcy. Any changes we make in Medicare will be to protect, preserve, and improve Medicare.

Our objective is not to reduce current Medicare expenditures. In fact, in every Medicare plan we will seriously consider, *Medicare spending will continue to increase*—just not as fast as President Clinton currently proposes. We propose to increase spending on every Medicare beneficiary from an average of $4,000 today to about $6,400 in 2002. Medicare's two public trustees— David Walker and Stan Ross, who hold no government office—emphasized that Medicare savings should not be considered for any other purpose, including comprehensive reform. In the 1995 *Hospital Insurance Trustees Report*, they wrote that "it is now clear that Medicare reform needs to be addressed as a distinct legislative initiative. . . . The idea that reductions in Medicare expenditures should be available for other purposes, including even other health-care purposes, is mistaken."

Underscoring the seriousness of the Medicare situation, the Medicare trustees—including Labor Secretary Robert Reich, Treasury Secretary Robert Rubin, and Health and Human Services Secretary Donna Shalala—said in the same report that "to bring the [Hos-

pital Insurance] program into actuarial balance even
for the first twenty-five years . . . either outlays would
have to be reduced by 30 percent or income increased
by 44 percent (or some combination thereof)."

In other words, Medicare's short-term fiscal health
requires one of two things:

- *immediately* increasing payroll taxes 44 percent; or

- Congress's *immediately* decreasing Medicare spending by 30 percent.

Clearly, these options are too drastic to be accepted
by the Congress or the American people, nor do they
begin to address the program's needs as it faces the
retirement of the baby boom generation. These measures—as drastic as they are—would ensure solvency
for only the next twenty-five years, at which point the
program would still be bankrupt. Given the sheer magnitude of Medicare's financing shortfall, bipartisan
cooperation is essential to establish needed, lasting
reforms to keep the promise of Medicare to future
generations. We think Medicare is too important, and
its crisis too great, to ignore the problem. We must
begin to put Medicare on a sound financial footing,
and we ought to do this on a bipartisan basis. We cannot allow partisan wrangling over the budget to endan-
ger Medicare's survival.

Our plan is to put Medicare on a separate legislative track from the budget. While Medicare will not
be taken "off budget," it is so important and its problems are so urgent that it will be dealt with separately

from the budget. Our course is exactly the one rec-
ommended by Medicare's two public trustees, who
asked that Congress deal will Medicare as a "distinct
legislative initiative."

Action on Medicare will run parallel to and occur
during the same time period as action on the budget.
It will not be delayed. The purpose would be to solicit
broad participation from a variety of experts and the
public in determining how to achieve changes to protect Medicare from its impending bankruptcy. There
must be a dialogue that allows as much participation
by the public as possible. By the end of the entire process, we will propose the changes necessary to preserve Medicare's solvency, incorporate them into the
entire budget, and pass it this year.

The most astounding phenomenon in the face of
the trustees' warnings is Present Clinton's silence.
The President has received warnings by his own
appointees not once but twice—in April 1994 and
again in April 1995. Yet he has not offered any ideas
for saving the Medicare program, nor has he shown
any inclination to discuss the issue. Indeed, President
Clinton has remained steadfastly silent. There is no
question that he was willing and eager to tackle health-
care reform, but his continued silence on Medicare
begs the question: if President Clinton would tackle
health reform for the private sector—where 85 percent of the people are covered and where premium
costs were reduced 1.1 percent—why is he silent on
a program that will start deficit spending in the next
nineteen months and will be completely unable to pay
benefits in seven years?

The focus of preserving, protecting, and improving Medicare will be market-based reforms. These reforms will expand the health-care choices of our seniors. They will also reduce Medicare inflation by encouraging greater cost-consciousness on the part of Medicare recipients and by requiring wealthy seniors to pay a larger share of the program's cost. In other words, we want to create a Medicare system that will provide better medicine at lower cost with more choices. Here are some of the reforms that we are investigating:

- *Offer our seniors a menu of health-care choices.* We will restructure Medicare to allow recipients to have a full range of health-care choices. These will include: enrolling in an HMO or receiving a health-care "voucher" to buy the kind of insurance they wish. Seniors choosing among these options would receive 95 percent of the age-adjusted per capita cost of conventional Medicare coverage.

- *Allow Medical Savings Accounts for senior citizens.* Another option we will allow and even encourage for our senior citizens is the Medical Savings Account (MSA). Under this option, Medicare would give $3,000 to the senior citizen which would be placed in a personal health care account, or MSA. Seniors would draw on that account to pay their first $3,000 of health costs during the year. If their health costs exceeded $3,000, Medicare would cover all further expenses. But if the senior citizen did not incur the full $3,000 of expenses, he or she could keep the remaining funds and spend or save it as they wished. This would empower seniors to have more control over their health dollars, encourage them to be more cost sensitive when visiting the doctor's office or the hospital, and allow them the opportunity to have extra cash income if they stay healthy.

- *Medicare now costs about $5,900 per recipient.* We can provide an MSA option for seniors at a cost of $5,600 per year, according to a 1995 study by the National Center for Policy Analysis. MSAs are thus a win-win situation for seniors, the taxpayer, and Medicare's future.

- *Institute proven market-based reforms.* Market-based reforms have reduced the inflation rate in private-sector spending to 4.7 percent. Medicare spending can increase one-and-a-half times faster than health-care spending in the private sector and the savings would, in seven years, result in Medicare being solvent and sustainable for at least another generation. The results would meet the Medicare trustees' solvency test. Medicare beneficiaries do not have to be— and will not be—coerced into mandatory health alliances such as those proposed in Clinton's 1994 health-care proposal. However, Medicare beneficiaries who choose to not participate voluntarily in HMO-like services should be allowed to benefit from part of the savings that would accrue to the Medicare system.

Solving Medicare's financial crisis demands the immediate attention of Republicans and Democrats in Congress. The process of achieving those reforms will be difficult, complex, and often tedious. Especially in the face of Clinton taking a walk on this critical issue, Medicare beneficiaries—current and future—expect us to get the job done, get it done right, and get it done soon.

A GOVERNMENT BY THE CONSENT OF THE PEOPLE

When the government spends your tax dollars unwisely in the many ways described above, it robs you and every citizen of their opportunity to achieve the American Dream. Our goal is to try to ensure that government in Washington starts spending your tax dollars as judiciously and carefully as you spend your own money. That's obviously a Herculean task.

President Clinton and Vice President Gore are right that we need to "reinvent" many federal programs that don't work very well anymore. But we need to go further than that. We shouldn't reinvent programs that never should have been invented in the first place. The old-guard Washington Establishment will almost certainly wage a ferocious campaign of opposition against most of the changes that we propose. That doesn't matter. What matters is whether we can rally the support of the American people behind our budget plan.

This is where we need your help. We want your suggestions about how to cut the deficit. What programs don't work? Where is there too much bureau-cracy or waste? How could government do things cheaper? Which of our ideas do you support? Which don't you agree with?

Let us know. Write Speaker Newt Gingrich or your representative with your ideas or complaints. Together, we can defeat the special interests, transform our government, and balance our budget.

6

Reenergizing the Economy

AFTER TWO-AND-A-HALF years of the Clinton presidency, we think it's fairly safe to conclude that Clintonomics is a bust. It was meant to reduce the deficit, but, as we've seen, despite some temporary improvement, the long-term budget outlook is as grim as ever. The financial hole is deeper now than before Clinton entered office, because we've squandered two years. Clintonomics was meant to reduce interest rates, but rates have risen substantially since the 1993 Clinton budget plan took effect. And it was meant to raise the incomes of average American workers. But in 1993—the first year of Clintonomics and the second year of the "recovery"—average family income declined by 2 percent, or by $709 dollars per family.

This leaves America without an economic game plan—at least without one quarterbacked by the White House.

In contrast, we do have an economic game plan and its central theme is to get bureaucratic government off of America's back and out of the way. Our commitment to ending deficit spending in Washington will be a key first step, of course, to reenergizing our economy. But we have to do more to spur economic expansion and opportunity for all our citizens than just combating the budget deficit. We think there are three other iron shackles bound tightly around the ankles of our domestic economy. They are taxation, regulation, and litigation. In order to have a first-rate, globally competitive world economy, we must liberate American workers and businesses from each of these burdens.

WHY GROWTH MATTERS

Throughout much of this century, America has experienced steady and robust economic growth. This constantly rising economic tide is what has made the American Dream a reality for so many tens of millions of our parents, grandparents, and great-grandparents. The Institute for Policy Innovation reports that for most of this century the economy has grown at a real rate of between 3.5 and 4 percent per year. This has meant that about every twenty-five years, the standard of living in the United States has doubled.

But now those growth rates of the past are said to be unattainable. The President's own economic projections have the economy trudging forward at only 2.5 percent per year—and even this is challenged by some experts as overly optimistic. In other words, America is now suffering from a long-run growth deficit.

What difference does this make? Why should we care that the economy is growing at 2.5 percent rather than the 3.5 percent we once expected? Here are several ways of looking at it:

• If we can make the economy grow one percentage point faster, Social Security will be saved and will remain solvent far into the foreseeable future.

• If we can make the economy grow one percentage point faster, family incomes will be $9,500 higher than otherwise after ten years. The American Dream will be as attainable for our children as it was for our parents.

• If we can make the economy grow one percentage point faster, the deficit will be reduced automatically by $640 billion over seven years. This would take us halfway to a balanced budget.

This last point is absolutely critical. It is often overlooked that the most painless way by far to reduce the budget deficit is to make the economy grow faster. This is why growth-oriented tax reductions, such as marginal rate reductions, regulatory roll-back measures, and common sense legal reforms are critical to our overall deficit reduction strategy. By the same token, if the economy continues to stagnate—perhaps because of high taxes, inflationary monetary policy, or more stringent business and labor regulation—more people will collect government welfare benefits and there will be fewer workers on the job collecting lower earnings. Tax revenues would dribble into the treasury. Under such conditions, substantial deficit reduction would be painful and difficult—maybe impossible.

Economic austerity is the adversary of deficit reduction. If we want a balanced budget, we *must* pursue other policies that will generate job and income growth. President John F. Kennedy eloquently made this point some thirty years ago when he unveiled his own tax cut plan: "An economy hampered with restrictive tax rates will never produce enough revenue to balance the budget, just as it will never produce enough jobs." This is precisely why we will pursue an ambitious agenda of economic growth initiatives. They are critical to our quest to reach a balanced budget by 2002.

TAXING THE AMERICAN DREAM

A founding principle of this nation was the idea of "no taxation without representation." The tragedy is that today, we have immeasurably more taxation with representation than we ever had without representation. The burden is rising all the time. For example, the graph on the opposite page shows the federal tax burden per household in 1900, 1950, and 1994. In 1995, the average household will pay nearly $20,000 in taxes.

We are pleased to announce that thanks to the successful passage of what House Speaker Newt Gingrich calls "the crown jewel" of our *Contract with America,* substantial tax relief is on the way. The *Contract* contained several tax initiatives, including the $500 family tax credit, expanded IRAs, incentives for business capital purchases, and a capital gains tax cut.

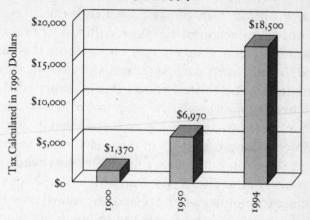

Real Total Government Taxes Per Household, 1900–1994

(Source: Institute for Policy Innovation, Lewisville, Texas, 1995)

A FAIRER AND SIMPLER TAX SYSTEM

As important as all the tax provisions of the *Contract* are for our families and our economy, we believe that they are merely transitional steps toward a comprehensive overhaul of our entire antiquated income tax system. Over the next eighteen months, we want to totally uproot our current 9,000-page tax code and replace it with a system that is fair, simple, and progrowth. Very few Americans would argue with the proposition that our current arcane and punitive federal tax system fails miserably on each of these counts.

Ask yourself: is the current tax system fair? Most Americans say no. Opinion polls reveal that about four out of five Americans don't like the current tax system.

Is the tax system simple? Not by a long shot. In 1990 American workers and businesses spent more than 5 billion man-hours computing their taxes. According to economist Walter Williams of George Mason University, this is more man-hours than are used to build every car, van, truck, and airplane manufactured in the United States. It represents a deadweight economic loss to the economy of at least $100 billion. The tax code is so convoluted that even the people in Congress who wrote the laws don't understand them. In 1992 *Money* magazine surveyed the members of the House Ways and Means and Senate Finance Committees—the two congressional tax writing committees—and found that more than 60 percent used professional tax preparers to figure out their personal taxes. We should all be able to agree that a tax system that's too complicated for the people who wrote the laws in Congress is too complicated for America.

Is the tax system oriented toward enhancing economic growth and prosperity? This is the area where our tax code fails us most dramatically. Each year hundreds of billions of dollars of output and income are lost simply as a result of our archaic tax policies. A recent study by Harvard University economist Dale Jorgenson documents the inefficiencies and anti-growth components of the current income tax code:

- Every additional dollar that is raised by Uncle Sam leads to a reduction of about 34 cents in national output.

- These inefficiencies cost the U.S. economy more than $200 billion in lost output each year.

- The United States could raise roughly the same amount of tax revenue as we do today but increase the incomes of the average American family by some $2,000 every year by simply moving toward a flatter, simpler, and less distorted income tax. Thanks to "soak-the-rich" tax hikes in recent years, the highest marginal income tax rate at the federal level today is 42 percent. When state taxes are included in the calculation, many individuals pay more than half of their earnings in taxes. Who pays these soak-the-rich taxes? Studies show that these high income tax rates apply in large part to small business owners—the major creators of new jobs in our society. Paradoxically, high tax rates designed to soak the rich have tended to reduce the amount of taxes the rich actually pay, and low tax rates increase tax payments by the rich. For example, in the 1980s, after Reagan cut income tax rates, the share of income taxes paid by the wealthiest 1 percent of Americans rose from 22 percent to 26 percent.

All of this leads us to this important conclusion: our current income tax system does not work for Americans of any income group. It is fundamentally broken. Tinkering will not fix the problem. The system needs total reconstruction. As such, over the course of the next several months we want to study two innovative alternatives: the flat tax and the national sales tax. We have already asked former Rep. Jack Kemp to head a federal study group to investigate these proposals and make recommendations to us in the fall.

THE FLAT TAX

The flat tax, sponsored by Majority Leader Dick Armey of Texas, would vastly simplify the tax system. It is quickly gathering a whirlwind of political momentum across America. Under the plan, all income would be taxed once and only once—at the single low rate of 17 percent. All tax deductions, loopholes, and credits would be eliminated—except for large personal allowances for workers, spouse, and children. For a single person, the first $13,100 of income would be tax free. For a family of four, the first $36,800 of income would not be taxed. All taxes on income from savings and investment, such as the capital gains tax and the inheritance tax, would be eliminated.

The flat tax has the following advantages:

• It makes the tax system so simple that Americans could fill out their taxes on a postcard and, in most cases, in less than twenty minutes.

• It lowers the tax burden on most Americans, particularly families with children.

• It is fair and progressive. The plan takes an estimated 5 to 10 million low-income working Americans off of the income tax rolls completely.

Form 1 ARMEY-SHELBY FLAT TAX FORM 1997		
Your first name and initial	Last name	Your social security number
Present home address		Spouse's social security number
City, Town or Post Office Box, State and ZIP code	Your occupation	
	Spouse's occupation	
1. Wages, Salary, and Pensions...	1	
2. Personal Allowance...		
a. $26,200 for married filing jointly...	2(a)	
b. $13,100 for single...	2(b)	
c. $17,200 for single head of household....................................	2(c)	
3. Number of dependents, not including spouse.............................	3	
4. Personal allowances for dependents(line 3 multiplied by $5300).	4	
5. Total personal allowances (line 2 plus line 4).............................	5	
6. Taxable wages (line 1 less line 5, if positive, otherwise zero).......	6	
7. Tax (17% of line 6)...	7	
8. Tax already paid...	8	
9. Tax due (line 7 less line 8, if positive).....................................	9	
10. Refund due (line 8 less line 7, if positive).................................	10	

• It promotes jobs and higher wages by lowering tax rates and eliminating the punitive treatment of savings and investment in the current code. As President Kennedy put it in 1963: "We must reinforce the American principle of additional reward for additional effort."

ABOLITION OF THE INCOME TAX

Another reform idea is also gathering steam in Congress and across the country: eliminating the income tax completely and replacing it with a national sales tax. Under this plan, there would be no tax on personal income, corporate income, or capital gains. April 15 would no longer be a day of dread. The IRS—and its 115,000 agents who are empowered to examine every aspect of our private affairs—would be dismantled. It would no longer be the government's business how much money you make.

Ways and Means Committee Chairman Bill Archer of Texas and Rep. Dan Schaefer of Colorado are independently developing plans to replace the income tax with a national sales tax. Studies indicate that to liberate America from the income tax and replace the revenue from the current system, a 17 percent national sales tax would have to be imposed. The plan could be made nonregressive by rebating to every American the tax paid on their first $5,000 of purchases each year. This would mean that a family of four with an income below $20,000 would pay no federal tax. The virtues of the national sales tax are:

• All savings and investments would be tax free. This would greatly enhance economic growth and capital flight into the United States. It will also end the punitive tax treatment of America's exports.

• Lower tax rates on all citizens would unleash the economic talents and energies of American workers and businesses. People who take risks and become successful could keep the fruits of their labor.

• The complexity of the tax system would be all but eliminated. No more tax returns. No more filing for extensions. No more costly and time-consuming record-keeping requirements.

- Americans would no longer live in perpetual fear and loathing of the most intrusive agency of government—the IRS. The agency would be all but eliminated. The states, forty-five of which already have a sales tax, could collect the tax with minimal increased enforcement burden (with Washington reimbursing them for whatever extra costs there might be, of course).

A TWENTY-FIRST CENTURY TAX SYSTEM

Will Rogers once quipped: "The income tax has made liars out of more Americans than the game of golf." We don't know yet what the ideal alternative is to the current federal tax system. But we do know that the current tax code is an archaic, convoluted, ugly mess. It is making America poorer. Almost no one—other than accountants, tax lawyers, lobbyists, and the Clinton administration—supports the tax code we now have in place. We are committed to changing the system, the only issue is: which change? Here again, we want to revamp our tax laws in close consultation with the American public. Which alternative do you prefer? Let us know.

THE REGULATORY STRANGLEHOLD

Isn't it about time we imposed some common-sense restraints on meddlesome federal regulators? Every year we have been adding more and more rules, regulations, and mandates on to the backs of American businesses, communities, and families. The economic consulting firm A. B. Laffer, Canto and Associates reports that in 1935 there were 4,000 pages in the federal register. Today there are 65,000. Stacked together, these volumes of regulation would reach to the top of the Washington Monument. For Washington's army of lawyers and lobbyists, all this red tape and regulation is good news; for the rest of us it is creating a national migraine headache.

These days, even liberals are starting to acknowledge that federal regulators are out of control. For example, when he was running for President as a "New Democrat," Bill Clinton correctly pointed out that "Expanding regulations threaten to overwhelm the nation's entrepreneurs and divert them from the task of building strong innovative companies." (But now he is threatening to veto our regulatory reform measures.)

Vice President Al Gore announced in his 1993 *Reinventing Government* report that regulations cost businesses and workers "at least $430 billion per year—9 percent of our gross domestic product." We think the cost is actually closer to $600 billion—but $430 billion is a towering number in any case. Even *The Washington Post*, in an editorial entitled GOOD MOVE ON REGULATION, endorsed the *Contract with America*'s regulatory provisions by saying: "The United States has become an over-regulated society. It is not just the volume or even the cost of regulation that is the problem, but the haphazard pattern—a lack of proportion. The government too often seems to be battling major and minor risks, widespread and narrow, real and negligible, with equal zeal. The underlying statutes are not a coherent body of law but a kind of archeological pile, each layer a reflection of the headlines and political impulses of the day. The excessive regulations discredit the essential. Too little attention is paid to the cost of the whole and the relation of the cost to benefit."

Increasingly, federal regulations border on the absurd. For example, the *National Review* reports that there are 66 words in the Lord's Prayer, 286 words in the Gettysburg Address, 1,322 words in the Declaration of Independence, but 26,911 words in the federal regulations on the sale of cabbages. How is it that these kinds of plainly inefficient regulations ever got enacted into law in the first place? One answer is that Congress has never been required to balance the cost versus the benefit when it passes new regulations. This is the equivalent of holding a trial, but only allowing one side to present its case.

Sometimes even the best-intentioned regulations spiral out of control. For example, many of us who were in Congress in 1990 voted for the Americans with Disabilities Act. The law is intended to protect the civil rights of the disabled by prohibiting discrimination in the workplace and requiring access in public buildings and facilities. Who could be against providing civil-rights protections and special accommodations for those in our society who are blind or in wheelchairs? But under the Act, 43 million people— that's one out of every six Americans—are potentially considered "disabled," though they may not know they are disabled themselves. The list includes drug abusers, the obese, and the "emotionally disturbed."

We don't know if we should laugh or cry over the latest nationally publicized incident involving the Act. The Associated Press reported earlier this year that Dade County, Florida, must spend $18,500 to build a wheelchair ramp to a nude beach and $30,000 more for handicapped parking spaces at the beach's lot. Civil-rights lawyers prevailed when they insisted that the ramp and parking spaces were required under the Disabilities Act.

These kinds of regulatory horror stories are becoming far too commonplace. Too many of Washington's one-size fits all regulations are senseless, arbitrary, and entirely insensitive to the huge cost they impose. For this reason, federal regulatory overreach reduces job opportunities. The economic costs of regulation are much higher than most Americans and federal policymakers realize. For example:

• Regulations add as much as 33 percent to the cost of building an airplane engine and as much as 95 percent to the price of a new vaccine. Federal regulation also adds about $3,000 to the cost of a new car.

• Excessive regulation has the impact of a tax on every American worker. It's estimated that regulation and mandates add about $6,000 to the cost of a business hiring a new worker. A report by the well-respected Joint Economic Committee of Congress found that these costs have risen by one-third since 1989 and likens their impact to "a form of economic crib death, suffocating jobs in the cradle of small business."

Our *Contract with America* was the first significant counterattack in some twenty-five years against unnecessary and inefficient regulation. We want to emphasize that the measures we put in place will *not* roll back the important and effective safety and environmental regulations that have a positive impact on our lives—notwithstanding the scaremongering campaign of our critics in Washington. We have all benefited from cleaner air and drinking water, a safer work environment, protection from unsafe drugs and products—and those laws that accomplish these objectives will continue to be vigorously enforced. No, our targets are the reams of regulations that do more harm than good. We want to separate the sensible regulations from the senseless.

Government regulations are meant to steer us from harm's way. And many, of course, do. But increasingly, as regulation has mushroomed into almost every area of our lives, the real danger to our well-being are the *regulators* not that which is regulated. To restore the American Dream we must put an end to costly and excessively burdensome regulations.

THE LITIGATION EXPLOSION

The third major impediment to creating a prosperous and growing economy is excessive litigation. Quite simply, America is overrun with lawyers and lawsuits.

America has four times as many lawyers per person as does Great Britain, five times more than Germany, ten times more than France, and almost twenty times more than Japan.

The ratio of lawyers to population was relatively constant at about 1,200 per million residents from the time of the Civil War through the Second World War. For all those years the American legal system worked well; indeed, justice was swifter, more certain, and much less costly than today. Over the last thirty years or so, the legal profession has multiplied nearly three-fold as a share of the population. Not coincidentally, the number of federal lawsuits also tripled from 1960 to 1990. In 1991 there were more than 18 million law-suits filed.

It should be no surprise that Washington, D.C., is a hornets' nest of lawyers. Washington alone has more lawyers than all of Japan. For many federal programs the largest cost is legal expenses. Take the Superfund program, for example. It is estimated that well over one-third of the $7.5 billion that has been spent since the early 1980s to clean up Superfund toxic dump sites have been swallowed up in legal and adminis-trative costs.

The litigation explosion is touching every area of our lives:

• Little League Baseball Inc., for example, com-plains that frivolous lawsuits, including one instance where a coach was sued when a player was hit by a pop fly, have driven liability insurance costs way up.

• *The Wall Street Journal* retold this story earlier this year: "After accepting a $2 million settlement for injuries allegedly suffered at a restaurant, Annie-Marie Leal rose out of her wheel chair and walked—in high heels."

• In 1992 a jury awarded $24,595 to a convicted mugger whose leg was broken after a taxi driver pinned him to the wall with his taxi while apprehending him.

All of these litigation horror stories merely underscore the real tragedy with the United States legal system today: despite having a vast wealth of attorneys and lawsuits, we have a dearth of justice. The legal system doesn't work well for ordinary citizens—though it imposes huge hidden costs on them. In 1992 the Bush administration's Council on Competitiveness issued a study concluding that "America is in the midst of a litigation explosion" and estimating that the cost of the lawsuit feeding frenzy in America is as much as $300 billion in direct and indirect costs a year. At least 20 percent of these costs, or $60 billion a year, are avoidable costs.

Our *Contract with America* instituted several legal reforms aimed at stemming the endless tide of litigation. The most important of these were:

• *Penalties for frivolous suits.* Requires attorneys who file frivolous suits or engage in abusive litigation practices with the aim of harassing or injuring the opposing party to compensate the victim.

- *Reasonable limits on punitive damages*. Caps punitive damage awards at $250,000 or three times the actual harm to the plaintiff.

- *Reform of product liability laws*. Limits the liability of product sellers to harm caused by their own negligence; limits the liability due to the injured party's misuse of the product; and creates sanctions for bringing frivolous liability suits.

Our intent is to unburden American businesses and citizens from the harassment and costs associated with excessive lawsuits. We want to discourage baseless suits so that substantive cases can be adjudicated swiftly and justly. We will continue to fight for final passage of the *Contract* provisions and continue to seek new remedies to unproductive litigation. If America is to retain its global economic competitiveness, we can no longer afford to have the most costly and inefficient legal system in the world.

LIBERATING THE AMERICAN ECONOMY

America cannot hope to resurrect the American Dream for all our citizens, cannot balance the federal budget once and for all, and cannot provide the global leadership for the Free World in the twenty-first century with an economy trudging forward at half speed. Too many of the old-guard entrenched powers in Washington are fully satisfied with a slowly growing America. This slow growth is the all-too-predictable product of years of misguided austerity measures imposed by government to protect narrow special interests and preserve bureaucratic empires.

We need to liberate America from the triple threat of excessive taxation, regulation, and litigation. Each is an enemy of the American Dream. Just as important, we need to resoundingly reject the slow-growth outlook. America and Americans can do better. As we move into what some have called "the third-wave information age," the United States can and should have the most rapidly accelerating economy in the world. We have the intellectual, institutional, and technological capability of dominating virtually every important information-based industry in the next century. All that has been lacking is bold, decisive, and visionary leadership in Washington. With your help and support, we intend to provide it.

7
Building an Opportunity Society

ISN'T IT TIME for Washington to start giving the disadvantaged in our society a hand up rather than a handout? Only government could spend $5 trillion over thirty years and wind up making more people poor. As Wisconsin Gov. Tommy Thompson recently observed of the welfare state, "The real tragedy is not how much has been spent, but how little progress has been bought."

The Great Society of the 1960s set out with admirable goals: to alleviate poverty, end the dole, repair broken families, and bring hope and dignity back to declining low-income communities. It has succeeded in making all of these problems worse—much worse. The poverty rate in America is higher today than it was thirty years ago, before the War on Poverty was launched. The American public does not need to be convinced of the failure of welfare. In the name of compassion we funded a system that is cruel and destroys opportunities. We all see its legacy reflected by the violence, brutality, child abuse, broken families, and drug addiction in every local nightly TV news broadcast.

The only real question is: how do we fix it? How can we bring an enduring spirit of hope and opportunity back into the lives of Americans trapped in the bondage of the modern welfare state—including, most essentially, the 18 million blameless children who now live in poverty? The short answer is that we need to first recognize that the government structures erected in Washington over the past quarter century must be entirely uprooted. It is not our goal to create a cheaper welfare state. It is not money we are trying to save— it's minds and lives. What we have in mind is a whole-sale transformation of the current crumbling and corrupting welfare-state system into a genuine opportunity society that opens doors to every American.

This new opportunity society will:

• Replace the current network of expensive, unco-ordinated and value-void, anti-poverty programs with work, family, and personal responsibility.

• Inject competition, choice, and discipline into our failing public-school system, particularly in low-income neighborhoods.

• Form a new federal partnership with urban America to bring capital and capitalism back to our struggling inner cities.

OUR VISION OF AN OPPORTUNITY SOCIETY

The opportunity society is a radical departure from the conventional approach in Washington toward solving society's problems. It does not try to tinker with the current structure, but instead recognizes it as financially and morally bankrupt. The welfare state is not fixable because the model is wrong at its very foundation. It needs to be replaced with a new structure emphasizing dignity, hope, and individual responsibility.

Here are the essential differences between the liberal Democratic model of the past three decades and the Republican opportunity model we envision for the future:

- The welfare state empowers bureaucrats to make decisions for the poor; the opportunity society empowers the poor to make decisions for themselves.

- The welfare state perpetuates an ethic of victimization; the opportunity society cultivates an ethic of personal responsibility.

- The welfare state relies on centralized command-and-control structures; the opportunity society relies on localized and market-based solutions.

- The welfare state rewards socially irresponsible behavior; the opportunity society encourages socially productive behavior.

- The welfare state ultimately creates a culture of dependency; the opportunity society replaces dependency with work.

OUT OF WELFARE, IN TO WORK

No program symbolizes the axiom of good intentions gone awry as fully as welfare. The welfare state was launched with great praise and promise as the centerpiece of Lyndon Johnson's Great Society agenda. The nation would "fight a war on poverty," Johnson declared. With great fanfare he announced that "the days of the dole in our country are numbered."

Roughly $5.1 trillion and 10,000 days later, the dole is more entrenched in modern American life than ever before. More than 35 million Americans receive some type of welfare assistance. This year, $300 billion will be spent on the War on Poverty, even though it would only require slightly more than one-third this amount of spending to bring every family in America above the poverty level if we were just handing out cash. We now spend more than $26,000 for every two-person family (an unwed mother and her child) on welfare. Yet there are still more than 30 million Americans— 15 percent of the population—who are classified as below the poverty level after we pass out all this money.

But the real tragedy of the welfare state is that it has ruined lives, families, and whole communities. The welfare system, as we see it, has:

• Encouraged illegitimacy. Since the invention of the modern welfare state in 1965, unmarried pregnancies have doubled. More welfare has meant more out-of-wedlock births—mostly to teenage girls unprepared financially and psychologically to handle parenthood.

• Fostered a culture of dependency. The graph below shows what Heritage Foundation welfare specialist Robert Rector has called "the poverty paradox." The paradox is that the $5 trillion avalanche of funds addressed toward fighting poverty has failed to budge the poverty rate downward. In fact, poverty fell rapidly from 1950 to the mid-1960s; progress was halted once the War on Poverty was launched.

• Penalized work. One of the most insidious effects of welfare is to make work financially unrewarding. The group Change NY found that a New York family

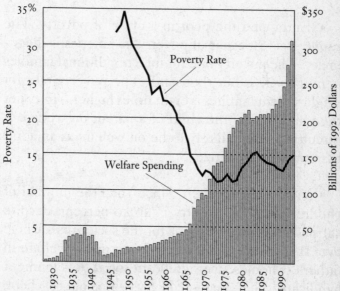

**The Poverty Paradox:
The Poverty Rate and Welfare Spending**

(Source: Heritage Foundation.)

on welfare receiving the whole range of public assistance benefits would have to find a job that paid a pre-tax income of more than $42,000 to compensate for taxes and lost benefits. In many other states the pre-tax income to compensate for the loss of all welfare would have to be more than $30,000. This means that many now on welfare would actually be poorer if they returned to work.

• Eroded our culture, our value system, and our families. No civilization can prosper with seventeen-year-old girls having babies who will grow up in broken homes without a father. The fruit of the welfare state—unmarried children having children—is a prescription for cultural suicide.

• Entrapped the poor in a cycle of poverty. The single greatest cause of poverty in America is illegitimacy. The poverty rate for intact traditional families is roughly five per thousand. The poverty rate for single-parent families is eight times higher—forty per thousand. Today the child of a parent on welfare is three times more likely to be on welfare as an adult than the average citizen.

• Victimized children. Since 1970 the number of children living in poverty is up 40 percent, despite substantial economic gains for the society as a whole over that period. Children growing up on welfare in fatherless homes face significant social-development handicaps. They are more likely to drop out of school;

they are more likely to use drugs; they are more likely to commit crimes.

The good news is that there is now nearly universal agreement that the welfare system is broken. As President Clinton put it: "We must revolutionize our welfare system. It doesn't work. It defies our values as a nation." He pledged to "end welfare as we know it." Unfortunately, this "New Democrat" rhetoric never translated into White House or congressional action—until this year.

ENDING WELFARE AS WE KNOW IT

What is the standard by which welfare reform should be judged? We have established the following goal for our overhaul of the federal welfare system: to turn formerly dependent, dispirited individuals once trapped on welfare into wholesome, productive citizens. To this end, our *Contract with America* is a hopeful and ambitious start. What the Democrats could not—or rather, would not—do in thirty years, we did in one hundred days. As expected, our critics savagely attacked our reform measures as unfair, but remember this: they had no alternative except to defend the status quo. And while the naysayers and the giant poverty industry in Washington sat on the sideline futilely defending the current welfare state, we enacted what *The New York Times* labeled "the most sweeping changes in the nation's social welfare system in sixty years."

Our welfare reform measures stress the following six principles, all of which we think the American public agree with.

1. Require work for benefits.
2. Turn back most of welfare to the states to encourage experimentation and cost-effectiveness.
3. Stop subsidizing illegitimacy.
4. Make welfare a temporary safety net, not a lifetime support system.
5. End the open-ended entitlement feature of welfare by block granting programs to the states and establishing enforceable spending caps.
6. Renew the vital role of private institutions such as charities, Boys and Girls Clubs, and neighborhood groups to serve as support networks.

The major provisions of the *Contract with America*'s Personal Responsibility Act would:

• Restrict welfare benefits to teenage mothers. Mothers under the age of eighteen may no longer receive any Aid for Families with Dependent Children (AFDC) cash payments for children born out of wedlock, and states can restrict such payments to mothers who are eighteen, nineteen, or twenty years old. Also, no additional payments will be made to women on welfare who have another child out of wedlock.

Currently, one-third of women on AFDC in California conceive another child while on welfare.

• Establish work requirements. States must begin moving welfare recipients into work programs after they have received benefits for two years.

• End a family's welfare payments after five years. Welfare will no longer be a way of life. We want the safety net to be a trampoline, not a hammock.

• Expand opportunities for states to develop their own welfare programs. The bill consolidates welfare programs into block grants to states giving them maximum flexibility to develop their own nutrition programs. States are also empowered to create their own work and training programs.

• Deny noncitizens most welfare benefits such as AFDC, Social Security, rental assistance, job training, and food stamps. The legislation makes exemptions for the aged.

Again, we view these changes as transitional. We believe most welfare—including AFDC, food stamps, public housing, and perhaps even Medicaid—should eventually be turned over to the states entirely. We are convinced that the puzzle of welfare dependency is much more likely to be solved through innovative state programs than from the centralized bureaucracies in Washington. States should be extended the full flexibility to fulfill their roles as "laboratories of democracy" when it comes to welfare. In fact, many states are already progressing with a torrent of promising reforms.

After a thirty-year experiment of spending $5 trillion on welfare—more than the entire cost of fighting both world wars, regrettably there's too much truth to the quip that "America fought a war on poverty, and poverty won." It's time to acknowledge failure and try bold new approaches.

FIXING OUR SCHOOLS

There is probably no greater threat to the American Dream than the inferior education the public school monopoly is providing our children. Almost every study over the past fifteen years on the quality of America's education confirms what Americans have come to know as true: that our schools deserve failing grades. The most devastating of these was the highly publicized 1983 report by the National Commission on Excellence in Education entitled *A Nation at Risk*. It warned that the "educational foundations of our society are presently being eroded by a rising tide of mediocrity" in America's schools.

That study is now twelve years old and everything we have learned since its release suggests that the tide of mediocrity is still rising. A 1988 report by the Carnegie Foundation for the Advancement of Teaching described city schools as "little more than human storehouses to keep young people off the streets." A 1992 International Assessment of Educational Progress report ranked American students thirteenth out of fifteen countries in their aptitude in science and math.

Other studies find that high percentages of our high-school graduates do not know what the *Federalist Papers* were, do not know what 9 percent of 100 is, cannot say within fifty years when the Civil War was fought, and cannot figure out a bus schedule. Seventy percent of Americans think that the quality of education is worse than it used to be—and they're probably right. In an age that rewards and demands productivity, our public school monopoly shows signs of *negative* productivity.

Make no mistake: if we continue to accept mediocrity from our schools and force parents to send their children to schools that don't teach, America cannot compete—and we certainly cannot win in the global economy of the twenty-first century. When we cheat our kids out of a first-rate education, we rob them of their opportunity to attain the American Dream and place severe limitations on their future careers.

If we could end the tragedy of our failing public schools by simply spending more money, this crisis would be easy and quick to solve. We in Congress would enthusiastically spend the money. So would American taxpayers: we are not a society that is stingy when it comes to spending money on improving the lives of our children. But regrettably about the only thing we know with certainty about the crisis in the public schools is that money will not solve the problem. If money were the solution, then America would have the best-performing schools in the world. Per-pupil spending in the United States is already higher than in Germany, Japan, France, the United Kingdom, and virtually all other developed countries. Of the major industrialized nations, only Switzerland spends more than the United States. Yet almost no nation gets less in return for its school dollars than we do.

The graph below shows the relationship between education spending and a standard measure of achievement—SAT scores—between 1970 and 1994. The chart calls into question whether the amount of money the schools are spending is at all related to how much our kids are actually learning. If anything, the spending/quality relationship appears to be negative.

More Educational Spending =
Sagging Educational Achievement

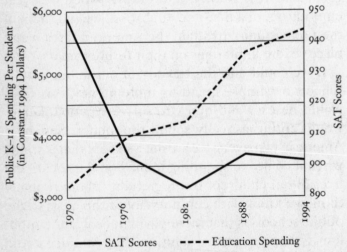

(Source: U.S. Education Dept., College Board 1995)

Real education spending has doubled in the past twenty-five years and nearly quadrupled in the past forty years. Today America spends about $6,000 per student in the public school system. Where did all this money go? The answer seems to be that it was swallowed up by the public-education blob. Incredibly, there are *twice* as many state and local education employees per student as there were in 1960 and *triple* the number as in 1940. We're not talking about teachers. These additional workers are school administrators, support staff, counselors, social workers, condom distributors, and so forth. Translation: most of the additional dollars devoted to the schools are intercepted before they ever arrive inside a classroom.

REDEFINING THE FEDERAL ROLE IN EDUCATION

What should be the federal government's role in education? Throughout most of our nation's history the answer to that question was easy: there was virtually no federal role in education. Before there was ever such a thing as a U.S. Department of Education, America generally had good, and in many cases, superb public schools. True, inner-city schools were not of high quality and had fewer resources, but the public school systems in places like New York, Chicago, Boston, Washington, D.C., are infinitely worse today than they ever were before there was federal involvement in education. It would be hard to argue that—other than from desegregation requirements—inner-city children have benefited in any tangible way from the federalization of education.

So what is to be done? First we have to acknowledge that years of conventional school reforms have failed. Throwing more money at a system that isn't working is the height of irresponsibility. The public school system in America—especially in the inner cities—has all the classic characteristics of failing institutions all over the world: it is command-and-control driven; it is monopolistic and severely limits customer choice; it entails massive bureaucracies; it is impervious to almost any market forces. In short, there is almost nothing about our current public school monopoly system and the federal role in helping finance it that is compatible with the principles of an opportunity society. Although we haven't settled on the ideal solution, House Republicans are considering several options, almost all of which would be an improvement over the current system:

Option 1: Close down the U.S. Department of Education.

Since 1978, the year the Department of Education was created to fulfill a campaign promise that Jimmy Carter had made to the politically powerful teachers' union, the federal government has spent $260 billion on the nation's schools. That money, in our view, has added virtually no value to the public school system across America. Rep. Sam Brownback and several dozen GOP House freshmen want the Department of Education to be shut down. Former Education secretaries William Bennett and Lamar Alexander have endorsed this option.

Option 2: Enact a Pell Grants program for parents of elementary and secondary-school children.

Currently the federal government provides about $10 billion a year in aid to elementary and secondary schools. If we continue this funding, rather than send the money to the education bureaucracies we could give out $2,000 education vouchers to parents of 5 million school-aged children. Allocation of these funds could go to parents with the lowest incomes first. The parents could then redeem these dollars at any public or private school they wished. For private schools with tuition costs of more than $2,000 a year, the parents would have to supplement the voucher with a payment out of their own income.

Why would this be preferable? Because it would empower parents—not bureaucrats. Parents would be given control of the education dollars for their children. This would offer parents much wider choices about where they want to send their kids to school. Especially for inner-city parents, this voucher could be a godsend. The well-respected Rand Corporation recently compared the achievement of students in the public and parochial schools of New York. It found that for about $2,000 less per student than the public schools spend, the New York City Catholic schools produce kids that on average perform one grade higher and have SAT scores that are 170 points higher than their counterparts in the public schools—even when socioeconomic backgrounds and other potential explanatory factors are controlled. The situation is identical in almost all our inner cities, according to the consensus of education researchers. The Catholic school system and most private schools in general (except for the very elite prep schools) provide a better education at half the cost of the public schools.

Today wealthy and upper-middle income families can and do escape the mediocrity of public schools by sending their children to private schools. That choice should be made available to parents of *all* incomes. Is this a radical idea? We have long allowed full choice—including religious schools—at the college level through the GI Bill, government scholarship programs, student loans, and Pell Grants. Thanks to the healthy forces of competition, America has the best university system in the world. Why not adopt the same model for our elementary and high schools?

Option 3: Allow experimental pilot voucher programs in the worst one hundred school districts in America.

With every fiber of its existence, the education bureaucracy will fight any reform that takes power from it and empowers parents with choices about where they send their kids to school. The education Establishment argues that vouchers will undermine the public school system. The bureaucrats seem to be doing a fine job of that without vouchers, but in any case, a more-limited voucher program may need to be instituted first. What if we took the one hundred worst-performing public school districts in America, and said that we would give $3,000 vouchers to the parents of kids trapped in these schools? No one could argue that these schools would be hurt, since it's unimaginable that these schools could perform any worse than they do already.

Under such a program, we would say to the low-income parents in these districts, "Here, we are giving you a $3,000 school voucher that you can use to send your child to any public or private school you wish. We think you can spend this money more wisely than Washington has." Would anyone disagree?

We could even go further. We might offer parents who are forced to send their kids to a school where a child has been injured with a gun, or where there is a well-founded fear of violence, a voucher to pull their kids out from under the cloud of terror. A recent national report found that there is an "epidemic of violence" in many inner-city schools. We don't think it's fair to force parents to send their children to a school where they have to worry each day about whether the kids are being assaulted, instead of how they did on their last test.

DEMANDING EXCELLENCE

Every child in America will be competing against today's children in Germany, China, and Japan when they reach adulthood. If American children are receiving an inferior basic schooling, no amount of federal job training can undo the damage. Improving America's education system is the key to reviving America's cities and reducing the gap between rich and poor.

For too long the education Establishment has invented a multitude of excuses for why our public school system is failing to perform. Historically this was a country that got the job done, that demanded excellence—not one that made excuses and invented scapegoats. Still, the education Establishment's awesome political power in Washington and across the country may thwart our efforts to inject the principles of an opportunity society into our school system. If they do, it will be a tragedy. There is perhaps no institution that needs basic reform more than our schools. To borrow a phrase from the United Negro College Fund, now more than ever "a mind is a terrible thing to waste." As a nation, we cannot afford to waste another single one.

BUILDING A NEW PARTNERSHIP

The failure of centralized bureaucratic planning is nowhere more evident than in our nation's big cities. Many of our once mighty and industrious central cities—New York, Chicago, Detroit, St. Louis, Philadelphia, Newark, to name a few—are bleeding to death. For more than a quarter-century, Americans have been voting with their feet against the liberal economic policies and decaying social conditions of these and other major American cities. Since 1965, fifteen of the largest twenty-five U.S. cities have lost a combined three million people, even while the total U.S. population rose by 60 million. Even middle-income minorities are now fleeing the cities in record numbers. Almost all quality-of-life indicators suggest a staggering decay of our inner cities:

- In Detroit, fathers are becoming an endangered species: two-thirds of the children there are reared in fatherless homes.

- Newark has a lower real per-capita income today than it did twenty-five years ago.

- The Chicago area has averaged 10,000 manufacturing job losses annually for the past fifteen years. A recent *Chicago Tribune* headline says it all: FACTORY FLIGHT HITS RECORD PACE.

- Washington, D.C., had some 500 violent murders in 1993 and now has been dubbed the "murder capital of the world."

- One of every seven New York City residents is on public assistance.

At a rally in Washington one month after the Los Angeles riots, then New York City Mayor David Dinkins described the inner cities as places of "only grief and despair." This may be true, but we believe there is no inevitability to the decline of our cities. The decline is a result of the failed legacy of liberalism: politically dictated, top-down, bureaucratic control from the center. Much of the fault lies with failed policies that cities have imposed on themselves, such as high taxes and suffocating regulations. But federal policies have contributed mightily to the demise of our cities as well.

HOW WASHINGTON HARMS CITIES

A bipartisan group of reform-minded mayors under the leadership of Republican Stephen Goldsmith of Indianapolis and Democrat John Norquist of Milwaukee has requested that House Republicans forge a "Contract with America's Cities." According to these mayors: "It is time for a total reconstruction of federal urban policy, founded upon five basic principles: citizen empowerment, choice, market reinvigoration, decentralization, and de-bureaucratization. What cities need from Washington are policies that foster vibrant markets not burdensome mandates. A 'stay-the-course' strategy will not contribute to the urban renaissance that we are convinced can be achieved with the help of more intelligent policy from Washington. Nor will the conventional call of urban leaders for a new multibillion-dollar, urban Marshall Plan. Unlike some of our colleagues, we're not asking Congress to write checks. Cities do not need more deficit spending from Washington. Our residents are federal taxpayers and like most Americans they are demanding greater value from Washington for their tax dollars." More federal money will not reverse the urban sclerosis of our inner cities. Since 1965 the federal government has spent

$2.5 trillion on cities. That is the equivalent of twenty-five Marshall Plans. The truth is that many policies out of Washington do harm to cities. The following federal policies erode the natural comparative advantage of cities:

• Unfunded mandates seem designed to destabilize city budgets.

• Ill-designed environmental and economic regulations are stifling inner-city redevelopment efforts.

• Public housing programs have long contributed to urban blight and have entrapped the urban poor in an environment of poverty, fear, and hopelessness.

• The massive federal budget deficit is crowding out private investment that could be taking place in cities.

• Federal welfare policies are expediting the decay of the moral infrastructure of cities by encouraging dependency and undermining individual responsibility, work, and marriage.

• Federal education grants seem to be designed to benefit the education Establishment more than inner-city children.

As Milwaukee Mayor John Norquist has stated, "Cities will never be rebuilt on fear and pity. An era of urban renewal will occur when city officials begin to fully implement more intelligent, market-based policies—and when Washington begins to do the same."

A CONTRACT WITH AMERICA'S CITIES

Rebuilding America's cities through smarter, market-based policies is one of our highest priorities in Congress. Forty million Americans live in the fifty largest central cities in the United States. They are vital resources that we must not leave behind as we enter the "third wave information age." So, as Mayors Goldsmith and Norquist have suggested, we pledge to enter into a contract with America's cities. We want to combine many of the policies that have already been enacted as part of the *Contract with America* with a new set of policies to aid cities. Here are six steps that would revitalize urban America:

1. *Establish a policy of no net new mandates imposed on cities*. A "time-out" on unfunded mandates to cities is long overdue. Currently, more than one-third of city budgets are devoted to complying with federal rules and regulations.

2. *Review existing federal mandates to find ways to reduce the cost burden on cities*. Cities have often been the major victims of the proliferation of federal regulations in recent years. Federal regulations which unnecessarily add to the cost of running cities include the Davis Bacon Act, the Clean Air Act, and the Superfund.

Washington must reform these laws in ways that will reduce costs to cities without undermining their basic missions. The Superfund, for example, imposes draconian cleanup standards on potential developers, even when they were not responsible for creating the waste in the first place. "This policy," as Mayor Goldsmith notes, "effectively quarantines many areas of our central cities."

3. *Convert the 106 federally designated urban enterprise zones into zero capital-gains tax centers.* The 106 federally designated enterprise zones represent just 1 percent of the land area in America and 2 percent of the population, but are home to one-third of America's poor. We have to find ways to bring investment back to these areas. We should end the bureaucratic grant-based "pork zones" established by the Clinton administration and instead declare all existing zones zero capital-gains tax centers to encourage new investment there.

4. *Replace the welfare state.* The culture of poverty perpetuated by the current welfare state—perhaps more than any other single factor—is devastating the physical, economic, and moral infrastructure of cities. A genuine culture of opportunity will take root in our cities, if we end welfare as we know it.

5. *Provide education vouchers to low-income parents in inner cities.* Cities are not inherently unsuitable environments for learning. After all, some of the best universities in the world are located in or around inner

cities—the University of Chicago, the University of Southern California, the University of Pennsylvania, and Columbia come to mind. Why then are these very same cities also home to some of the world's worst elementary and secondary schools? The problem with the elementary and secondary schools is that they act as a monopoly. Low and moderate income inner-city parents should be allowed to choose the best school—public or private—for their children.

6. *Downsize Washington and allow city residents to keep their dollars at home.* Many major cities are losers in the federal redistribution game. Residents of New York City, for example, send more tax dollars to Washington than they get back. For this reason we are convinced that cities will be major beneficiaries of our commitment to balance the federal budget by downsizing Washington. Whole Cabinet agencies—the departments of Education, Energy, and Commerce, for example—are of no consequence to cities. Hundreds of smaller federal programs fall into the same category. Cities will be better off without them.

We believe that the federal government can—indeed, must—help rebuild America's cities. Washington has an obligation to help resuscitate cities, if only because so many destructive federal policies of the past, such as welfare, created the devastation of urban America in the first place. The past generation of federal aid to cities seems to have been predicated on the elitist notion that federal lawmakers have a better idea of what's good for cities than do city leaders and residents themselves. If we have learned nothing else from misspending $2.5 trillion on cities over the past quarter century, it is that federal strategies to aid cities based on the one-size-fits-all approach are doomed to continued failure.

Our contract with America's cities will be based on the idea that residents of the nation's cities should be granted the maximum freedom to solve their own problems their own ways. We want to start empowering people living in cities—especially the poorest residents—not the bureaucrats living in Washington. One thing is certain: there can be no genuine American renaissance if the tens of millions of inner-city residents continue to be left out and left behind. We must bring the promise of the American Dream back into the home of every resident of every inner city, from the South Bronx to East Los Angeles. That is the central challenge of creating an opportunity society.

8

Strengthening the American Family

THE MOST VITAL investment that we can make in America's future is our children. Inside Washington there is a socially destructive, liberal mindset that government is the ultimate caretaker of America's children. Over the years the federal government has launched a bulky catalogue of programs on behalf of kids—and at the same time has imposed a heavy tax burden on families to pay for those programs. This is the essence of the "government-as-caretaker" philosophy that has gone unchallenged for many years in Congress.

In the real world, beyond the Washington Beltway, everyone knows that the real investment and sacrifice on behalf of children is not made by government do-gooders, educrats, congressmen, or social workers. The real investment and sacrifice is made by parents.

Big government is the adversary of the American family. There are countless ways that federal policies actually work against the family and against children. Here are some prominent examples:

• *High taxes place a crushing financial burden on families with children.* Taxes are now the single largest expense in a middle-income family budget.

- *Welfare subsidizes family breakdown.* The welfare state encourages illegitimacy and discourages marriage.

- *Our government education policies grant parents little role in the schooling of their children.* Many parents, because of low income, are denied the option of deciding where to send their kids to school. Moreover, the public school systems, through such policies as condom distribution, undercut values, such as abstinence, that parents try teach at home.

- *Federal budget and tax policies discourage parents from saving for their children's future.* Our income tax policies penalize parents who try to save for the purchase of a first home or education expenses, or to build equity in a family business.

- *The huge budget deficit is placing massive future financial burdens onto the backs of our children.* Budget deficits pass the cost of government programs onto the next generation. Children born today will face a lifetime tax burden of 80 percent or more if we do not change course.

Our *Contract with America* and our balanced budget plan will eliminate much of the anti-family bias of federal programs. This chapter describes the policies in our overall economic plan designed to strengthen the family. Without stable, loving, financially secure families, the American Dream will remain in jeopardy.

FAMILIES IN CRISIS

Much of this book has concentrated on solving the economic crises confronting this nation. But we are well aware that Americans are concerned about much more than just dollars-and-cents issues. They are worried about the breakdown of values, civility, and family structure. What are these moral problems that the public worries about? They see that crime rates have more than doubled in thirty years and that a record amount of this crime is committed by juveniles. They see alcohol and drug abuse still at high levels—particularly among teenagers. They see that one out of every four children in America today does not have a father in the home. They see that teenage out-of-wedlock pregnancies have reached an all-time high. In addition, they see a general lack of civility and respect in the way we treat each other.

For a quarter century or more, we have tried to combat these trends through bigger government—what we call "the nanny state" approach. We think a new approach is in order, one that centers on the concept of encouraging stable and constructive families. The family is the mechanism through which we transmit moral values, discipline, knowledge, and civility to our children. No matter how well-intentioned and well-conceived government programs might be, they can never serve the role of a substitute parent to transmit these values. Efforts to make our schools, our welfare programs, or our hundreds of other social programs perform the function of replacement parents are not only futile, they are dangerously counterproductive. All too often these programs contradict the very values that parents attempt to instill at home.

In short, the surest and swiftest way to overcome our moral problems in America is by strengthening the family. And the surest and swiftest way to strengthen families is to make sure that government stops punishing them.

WELFARE DESTROYS FAMILIES

The failed welfare state is at the center of so many of America's economic and social problems today. Consider what Sen. Daniel Patrick Moynihan, the liberal New York Democrat, said about the problem of social decay in a famous article published thirty years ago: "A community that allows a large number of young men to grow up in broken families, dominated by women, never acquiring any stable relationship to male authority, never acquiring rational expectations about the future—that community asks for and gets chaos."

The situation he described is the very byproduct of the modern welfare state. Since Moynihan wrote his report, the percentage of children born to broken families has more than quadrupled. In 1992 there were 1.2 million out-of-wedlock births—an illegitimacy rate of 22 percent for whites, 68 percent for blacks, and 30 percent for the nation as a whole. We are on the socially suicidal path of becoming a nation of dysfunctional families. The chaos Sen. Moynihan predicted is nearing our doorstep.

Welfare's worst effect has been to financially reward family disintegration. The three general conditions for receiving cash from the major welfare program, AFDC, are that you (1) must not work, (2) must not marry, and (3) must have a child for whom you cannot provide. These three conditions create unproductive economic incentives. But what is much worse is that these welfare policies transmit perverse moral signals. The welfare state says to the teenager: it is okay to have children out of wedlock, and if you do, we will take care of you and your child. We should be sending precisely the opposite message to young men and women. To wit, bringing a child into the world that you are neither emotionally nor financially prepared for is wrong and grievously irresponsible. It victimizes the innocent child. Illegitimacy and welfare are closely connected as the graph on the next page illustrates.

Children born into welfare face virtually every conceivable social development handicap. They are more prone to do poorly in school, suffer emotional problems, commit crimes, and to fall into poverty and welfare themselves when they reach adulthood.

Welfare reform doesn't punish children, welfare does. Strong, nurturing families and the modern welfare state simply cannot coexist. One will have to give way to the other. Our strategy is to elevate families and fix welfare.

The *Contract with America's* welfare reforms which we passed were designed to reduce the evil epidemic of illegitimacy and teenage pregnancies. Three reforms would help accomplish this:

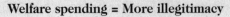

Welfare spending = More illegitimacy

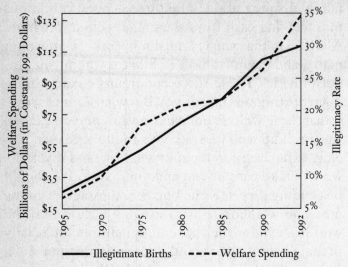

(Source: OMB, HHS, 1994)

- To discourage teenage pregnancies, the *Contract* prohibits AFDC payments and public housing assistance to unwed mothers under age eighteen. States have the option of extending this welfare prohibition to unwed mothers who are eighteen, nineteen, or twenty years old.

- To discourage mothers already on AFDC from having additional children they cannot afford to care for, the *Contract* ends the increase in AFDC benefits when additional children are born out of wedlock.

- To force fathers to take greater responsibility for their illegitimate children, the bill requires mothers to establish paternity as a condition for receiving AFDC

194

and strengthens child-support enforcement to require fathers to pay for the rearing of these children.

A PRO-FAMILY TAX CODE

Once upon a time America had a family-friendly tax system. Families paid little of the tax burden because society recognized that the first financial priority of parents should be to take care of their children and not their government. Not so anymore. Now taxes, at 40 percent of personal income, are a family's number-one monthly expense.

In the early 1950s the average family of four paid only about 5 percent of family income in taxes to Uncle Sam. Most of the rest was take-home pay. But in the 1990s, that same family pays roughly 24 percent of its earnings in federal income and payroll taxes. It is no coincidence that as the tax burden has gone up, family time has gone down. Studies show that parents today spend about 20 percent less time with their kids than did parents forty years ago. Social changes account for some of this decline in family time, but the heavier tax burden does too. Higher taxes mean that parents have to be out working more to earn enough to care for their family.

What if taxes on families were the same today as they were in the 1950s? How much in savings would this mean for a family? The answer is that if a family paid 4 percent rather than 24 percent of its income in taxes, its take-home pay would be roughly $10,000 a year higher than it is now!

There are two major reasons that taxes on families have risen appreciably over recent decades. First, the Social Security payroll tax has exploded from 6 percent to 15 percent of payroll for most families. Second, the tax exemption for children has been eroded by inflation over time. For the child exemption to be worth what it was to a family in 1948 it would have to be raised from $2,400 to almost $8,000 per child.

Now for some good news. For all the parents across America who are feeling grievously overtaxed, we are happy to report: relief is on the way. Here's what we've done:

> to make the tax code more family-friendly we approved a $500 tax credit per child for every family with an income below $200,000.

Predictably, this family tax cut came under fire from big-spending liberal Democrats who argued that Washington could not afford to lose the tax dollars it collects from these families. They also said that it was a tax giveaway to the rich. The facts show otherwise:

- The $500 credit eliminates taxes for 4.7 million poor working families.

- The families of 52 million American children will receive the credit.

- The reduction in taxes is skewed heavily in favor of low-income working families. Of the total tax cut, 74 percent of the benefit accrues to families with incomes below $75,000. Only 10 percent of the benefit goes to families with incomes above $100,000. See chart below.

• The tax cuts we approved did not increase the deficit by one dime. We cut government spending by more than the amount of the revenue reduction.

We would also note that in approving the $500 child tax credit liberal Democrats are now denouncing, we have delivered in less than one hundred days on a promise that Bill Clinton made nearly a thousand days earlier (but never delivered on)—his campaign pledge to provide middle-class tax relief. In fact, it was candidate Bill Clinton who said in his campaign document *Putting People First:* "Virtually every nation recognizes the importance of strong families in its tax code. We should too."

Who Benefits from the Family Tax Credit?

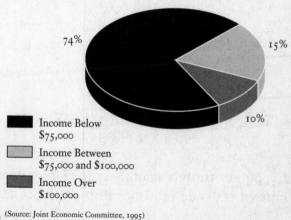

(Source: Joint Economic Committee, 1995)

The end result of our $500-per-child tax cut is to take money out of the hands of the federal bureaucrats and return it to the parents—who earned the money. Our argument for the $500 credit comes down to this: if you go out to work and you earn the money, should you as a parent spend the $500 on your kids, or should a bureaucrat? We choose the parents.

REFORM THE MARRIAGE PENALTY

Should our tax system discourage couples from getting married? Currently it does just that through what is known as the "marriage penalty." Under current law, a couple living together earning $40,000 each would pay $1,285 more tax if they got married than if they remained single. All told, marriage costs millions of Americans roughly $2 billion in higher taxes each year. That makes for expensive wedding vows! Our *Contract with America* repeals the marriage penalty:

> We provide a tax credit to married couples to begin eliminating the tax code's "marriage penalty."

THE AMERICAN DREAM SAVINGS ACCOUNTS

In our opinion, thrift is a family value. Unfortunately, our current tax code punishes thrift by twice taxing any money Americans save. Americans are taxed on the money when they earn it, and they are taxed on any proceeds, such as interest income, they receive when they save it. Given these savings disincentives, it should be no great surprise that America's savings rate is anemic. We are last of major industrial countries, at an annual household savings rate of 4.6 percent, behind Canada (10.8 percent), Britain (11.5 percent), Germany (12.3 percent), France (14.1 percent), and Japan (14.8 percent). The United States saves at half the rate of Europe and one-third that of Japan. A 1994 Merrill Lynch study shows that baby boomers, on average, are saving at only one-third the rate they should be in order to have a financially secure retirement.

Saving money is the traditional route through which families pursue and capture the American Dream. Family savings are used for college expenses, a new home, investment in a family business or farm, and the like. But today that dream is in jeopardy because half of American families have less than $1,000 in financial assets.

In the 1980s one of the ways that Americans built up savings was through Individual Retirement Accounts (IRAs). Nearly 16 million Americans took out IRAs in 1986. Three-quarters of the IRA contributions were made by families with incomes of less than $50,000. Unfortunately, as part of the 1986 tax law changes, stiff restrictions were placed on IRAs. In 1990, the number of IRAs was down to 6.5 million—more than a 50 percent decline. In dollars the slide has been even steeper. In today's dollars, Americans made $50 billion of investments in IRAs in 1986. Now only $8 billion a year is put into these savings accounts.

In order to encourage greater thrift, we not only want to bring back the IRA eligibility to all Americans, we want to expand IRA's attractiveness by allowing the funds to be drawn out for specific investments that families make in their future. Therefore, we have passed legislation that will create a new American Dream Savings Account, which allows all American families to make an IRA contribution of up to $2,000 for each spouse—including a spouse who is a homemaker. Money could be withdrawn from the American Dream Savings Account tax-free if used for (1) retirement income, (2) purchase of a first home, (3) college expenses, or (4) medical costs.

A PRO-FAMILY CONTRACT WITH AMERICA

Our *Contract with America* was above all else a pro-family set of public policy prescriptions. In addition to those mentioned above, the *Contract* contained several other new laws that will benefit families and children. These laws would:

- Facilitate adoption by providing a tax credit of up to $5,000 to cover adoption expenses.

- Provide a $500 tax credit for families caring for an elderly parent or grandparent.

• Establish stiffer penalties for sex crimes against minors and tougher child pornography laws.

• Expand parental rights by granting parents the right to supervise their children's participation in federally sponsored programs.

BALANCING THE FEDERAL BUDGET TO INCREASE THE FAMILY BUDGET

By far the most critical step we can take to protect and strengthen families, and especially children, is to honor our commitment to balance the federal budget by reducing the cost of government. When the government borrows $200 billion a year, it crowds out investment that families could be making in their own future. For example, the federal budget deficit may add as much as $75,000 in borrowing costs over the life of a $150,000 thirty-year home mortgage.

Every year that we continue to waste money in Washington on failed centralized bureaucratic programs, we rob every family budget of thousands of dollars. Contrary to the constant chatter in Washington about the need for government to "invest" more in our children, the reality is just the opposite. We need to allow parents to invest more in their children— and we need to get government to stop taking so much of their money. The single greatest investment that the American society can make in our children is to substantially cut back on the wastefulness and intrusiveness of government. The $24,000 a year that government now spends per family is, quite simply, not money well spent.

The longer we delay in balancing the federal budget, the further we imperil our children's future. If we simply allow government to run on automatic pilot and refuse to seize control of our economic destiny, then our young children will pay an expensive price tag—perhaps as much as 80 percent of their earnings in taxes—for our fiscal malfeasance. We refuse to leave that kind of financial legacy for our children. Therefore, we pledge to

> Increase the financial security of American families and the economic opportunities of their children by balancing the budget, regaining control of entitlements, and rooting out the epidemic of wasteful spending.

Our critics complain that we need more of Washington's social programs to help children. We believe that the only fully effective social program in America is the family. Two loving and nurturing parents are worth a thousand federal social workers. This is why the only way to truly restore the American Dream for our children is to start putting families first.

9
Empowering Citizens, Communities, and States

THE OVERRIDING ECONOMIC lesson of the past half century is clear: central planning is a failure. As we move into the next century, the top-down, command-and-control organizational structure is being tossed into the dust bin of history. Central planning didn't work in the Soviet Union, it didn't work in Eastern Europe, and it no longer works in major corporations. And now, with every passing day, it's becoming clearer that bureaucratic central planning is a bankrupt model—financially and intellectually—in Washington, D.C.

To transform the $1.6 trillion public enterprise in Washington into a citizen-responsive, cost-efficient operation, we must topple its massive bureaucratic structures and instead return money and power back to states, communities, and citizens themselves. We have to recognize that Washington's giant agencies are outdated marble relics of the past. They are irrelevant to the basic daily problems and concerns of Americans. To make the federal government work better at less cost, we need to ask ourselves some basic questions about what government in Washington can and cannot do for ordinary Americans. For example:

- Are struggling inner cities or their low-income residents really helped by having 10,000 bureaucrats thinking about their problems hundreds of miles away in the Housing and Urban Development Department?

- Are America's farmers made more productive because there are 110,000 workers at the Agriculture Department, most of whom are in Washington?

- Are American families better off when they send their tax dollars to Washington to support a sprawling Department of Health and Human Services agency? Are the poor?

- Do American workers get any measurable value from the $30 billion in tax dollars that are snatched from their paychecks and lost in a maze of cavernous corridors at the Labor Department?

- How many roads, bridges, and highways have been built by the thousands of administrators at the Transportation Department?

- Are school children sitting behind desks in classrooms across America really learning more as a result of there being 4,000 federal workers sitting behind desks at the Education Department?

To balance the budget we need to recognize that many of these bureaucratic empires in Washington are hopelessly obsolete—they are running against the natural course of history. Moreover, they contradict virtually every modern rule of efficient organization.

The genius of our Founding Fathers was to establish a federal system under which rights were constitutionally retained by the people and the states. Two hundred years ago the architects of our Constitution, with great foresight, rejected the concept of a one-size-fits-all centralized government system. That is, they rejected what our government has become today. The United States is predicated on the idea that Americans and their local communities are best suited to solving their own problems, their own ways. It is the recognition that what is best for South Dakota may not work in the South Bronx.

The message is clear: to make government work better and to balance the federal budget, we must now reverse the direction of the mighty river of power that for thirty years has been flowing away from the people and toward Washington. "Getting Washington out of the way," says Michigan's Gov. John Engler, "is the crucial first step in the long process of returning authority and responsibility where they belong—to our families and neighborhoods, churches and charitable organizations."

We agree. Bureaucracy and waste in Washington are the enemies of the American Dream. Let's try a new approach: returning power to the people.

Our *Contract with America* and now our fiscal blueprint for a balanced budget includes a three-step strategy to achieve a more fiscally responsible government in Washington and more direct citizen involvement in solving problems. The pillars are:

- *Shrink the bureaucracy in Washington.*

- *Return power to states and communities.*

- *Empower citizens to have more direct control over their government.*

The basic idea here, of course, is as old as America itself. It is the once revolutionary concept that the creativity, compassion, and enterprise to help solve community problems reside deeply within the individual citizen, not the state. Private initiative is what has propelled America to greatness, not collective action. In the 1800s French observer Alexis de Tocqueville marveled at how Americans relied on private associations "to found seminaries, to build inns, to construct churches, to diffuse books . . . to found hospitals and schools." For too long, the genius of individual and community-based initiatives like these have been smothered by the empty solutions of centralized government action.

STEP ONE: SHRINKING THE WASHINGTON BUREAUCRACY

With the fall of communism and the Soviet Kremlin, the United States government may now be the most overly bureaucratized institution in the world. The growth of bureaucracy at every level of government has been staggering. There are now 3 million civilian workers employed by the federal government. When local and state public employees are added to this total,

America now has more workers employed by government than our entire manufacturing sector.

Washington certainly doesn't need this many people. *The Wall Street Journal* recently published a report by an anonymous federal worker complaining of the culture of waste and bureaucracy in federal agencies. She noted that many federal employees routinely leave "solitaire"—the world's greatest time waster—on their computer screens when they leave their desks. Suffice it to say that these "workers" aren't helping Americans solve their problems—they're adding to them. There are certainly thousands of dedicated federal employees who work hard and productively. The problem is that Congress has made no effort in the past to separate the wheat from the chaff.

Bureaucracies flourish like bacteria inside the nation's capital. One example is the Bureau of Mines (BOM). In 1911 there were 800,000 miners in the United States. Over the last eighty years mining techniques have become much more efficient; today there are only 200,000 miners. But these efficiency gains have been lost on the folks at the BOM. The agency now has far more employees, 2,000, and spends several times more money, $175 million, than eighty years ago when mining flourished. The truth is that BOM could do its job with one-tenth the budget and the personnel.

The situation at the Agriculture Department is even more astonishing. The number of farmers in America fell by 70 percent, from 23 million in 1950 to 4.5 million in 1990. But the number of USDA employees grew by 53 percent over the same period. An agency that first started as a simple data-gathering center with a few hundred workers now employs 110,000 people. Because farming is more efficient and employs fewer people, USDA field offices have had to invent new missions, such as offering training courses in gourmet cooking and urban gardening. America has by far the most technically advanced, productive, and profitable farmers in the world. It's hard to imagine that farmers in Kansas, Iowa, and California wouldn't be even more productive without 110,000 federal government busy-bodies advising them on how to run their farms.

The Agriculture Department almost seems efficient when compared to the enormous social-services industry we've erected in Washington. *The Washington Post* reported in 1994 that "the cost of running welfare programs is rising twice as fast as the number of people on the rolls." From 1987 to 1991 Washington provided assistance to 18 percent more recipients but its administrative costs rose by 43 percent. Government audits reveal that Washington spends $6 billion to $8 billion a year in welfare's administrative costs alone. What difference does it make that we have this ocean of waste? With the upwards of $8 billion we waste on bureaucracy in the welfare state we could purchase thirty-five-foot yachts for 75,000 welfare recipients every year and still have money left over to reduce the deficit!

A research group in Wisconsin recently tried to determine how many of Washington's welfare dollars ever get spent on Milwaukee's poor. What the group found was that a tangled web of federal, state, and local anti-poverty bureaucracies has been gobbling up 65 cents of every welfare dollar before it ever reaches their intended destination. Milwaukee spends about $1.1 billion of federal, state, and local money annually on poverty abatement. This money flows through sixty-eight low-income assistance programs that spend an average of almost $30,000 per family in poverty. Now we know why this money is lifting so few families out of poverty—it never gets to them. It would appear that many people have gotten rich off the $5 trillion we have spent on welfare over the last thirty years. We only wish some of them had been poor people.

Layers Upon Layers of Waste

Then there is the related problem in Washington of program duplication. The federal government's sprawling bureaucracy has become so enormous that Uncle Sam's left hand is oblivious to what his right hand is doing. There are now 500 separate federal programs to provide aid to cities. Are they helping the inner-city poor or city finances? It's doubtful. According to Dallas Mayor Steve Bartlett, "Many of the federal aid programs are of little value to city officials or residents because of the regulatory strings attached and lack of flexibility in terms of how the funds can be spent." Bartlett says cities would gladly take less money from Washington if "we could spend the dollars as we wished."

Federal retraining programs are praised in Washington as the solution to unemployment for laid-off workers. Yet the headline of a recent *Wall Street Journal* front-page investigation on how well these programs work (or, rather, don't work) tells the real story of why job training is so popular in the nation's capital: JOB PROGRAMS FLUNK AT TRAINING BUT KEEP WASHINGTON AT WORK. The story notes there are over 150 training and education programs spending more than $24 billion a year. How are the dollars used?

• There are thirty-five separate programs for the disabled, sixty-five for the poor, and more than a dozen for veterans. "No area better illustrates Washington's sprawling, redundant bureaucracy than job training," observes the *Journal*.

• The Job Training Partnership Act, the largest of all federal training programs, "actually led to lower wages for poor young men compared with a control group."

• The Job Corps program costs $20,000 per recipient—roughly the annual tuition at Harvard.

These aren't just isolated examples. The list below documents the endless redundancies in federal agencies.

Activity	*Number of programs*
Job training programs	163 (in 15 different agencies)
Welfare programs	64
Education programs	240
Early childhood programs	93

Youth development	46
Urban aid	500, at least
Economic development	300, at least
Health professions education	42
Export promotion	10
Business support programs	71
Housing for the poor	60
Food safety	10

Is this wise use of our tax dollars? Wouldn't it be sensible and cost-effective to coordinate each of these activities within one or two programs? Costs would have to fall if all job training were consolidated under one roof, all education programs under another, and so on. And services would probably improve for recipients as well.

The Cost of Bureaucracy

Rep. Lamar Smith of Texas has long made it a personal crusade to root out the wasteful overhead and excessive personnel in government agencies. He has found that 15 to 20 percent of the federal tax dollars we send to Washington are eaten up in bureaucratic costs. That's more than double the overhead costs typical in private industry. When Rep. Smith recently tallied the total federal overhead costs of government, he came up with $270 billion a year. How much waste is this? It's more money than is in the entire budget of France. It's more money than the entire combined incomes of the residents of fourteen states.

More than $7 billion of this administrative expense is for travel. Admittedly, there are many legitimate reasons for federal employees to travel in and out of Washington on government business. But the House Budget Committee recently discovered that in the last month of the fiscal year, travel expenses increase by 50 percent over each of the previous eleven months. Why? Because agencies eagerly use up every last dime of their travel allowance rather than turn over an unused dollar to the taxpayers.

We are committed to rooting out bureaucratic waste in Washington as a critical step to ending deficit spending. The public enthusiastically supports such an effort. But make no mistake about it, the liberal Establishment will fight us every inch of the way.

Even in recent years of declining health-care inflation, Medicaid remains a recurring nightmare of stampeding costs. The program expanded by 13 percent in 1989, 18 percent in 1990, 30 percent in 1991, 21 percent in 1992, and 20 percent in 1993. Since 1989 Medicaid has grown at *five times the rate of inflation*. This Olympian achievement is due to sheer fiscal incompetence. Even *The Washington Post*'s recent feature on the history of Medicaid noted wistfully that "it seems clear the federal government has lost control of this program." Today one-third of all births are paid for by Medicaid.

The federal government has proven itself incapable of slowing the rampant inflation of Medicaid. But states are finding workable solutions to the crisis. Arizona, Ohio, and Wisconsin have been experimenting with managed-care options and have succeeded in chopping their Medicaid inflation rate in half. We want to encourage state flexibility, experimentation, and cost containment by converting Medicaid into a block grant to the states with minimal strings attached. Then we will cap the growth of federal payments to about 5 percent or 6 percent per year. If states can hold down costs, they can keep the difference. This proposal, which the governors have requested, would save the federal government about $150 billion over seven years.

We learned this lesson earlier in 1995 when we enacted our reforms to shift school lunch programs back to the states through a block grant, which would *increase* funding by 4.5 percent per year. The Washington Establishment engaged in a full-court press to frighten the public and exploit children. The current method of operation for this program is nonsensical. To wit, a clerk at a local school, who doesn't cook anything, checks off a report and sends it to the state clerk, who doesn't cook anything, and checks off a report and sends it to an office in Washington, where a worker who has never been in the county or perhaps even the state, examines the report written by two other bureaucrats. That's the bureaucratic model to make sure a child is eating right. That is the model we reject. We think local schools could feed thousands more children if we cut out the Washington middleman entirely.

STEP TWO: TURN POWER BACK TO THE STATES AND COMMUNITIES

To solve many of society's most intractable problems today, we need to concede that Washington doesn't have the answers—and in some cases isn't even asking the right questions. Even *The New York Times* recently questioned the wisdom of continuing to look toward Washington for policy solutions to social problems. The *Times* noted: "Despite trillions of dollars spent over the years on thousands of different government social programs, politicians are no closer today than they were a generation ago about the best ways to lift people out of poverty and make the cities a better place to live." That, in our opinion, is a chilling indictment of the status quo. States and localities don't have all the answers either, but they have critical advantages over the federal government in problem solving. These advantages include:

- They are closer to the people they are serving.

- They are more open to experimentation.

- They are generally less mired in red tape, regulation, and hierarchical chains of command.

- They are able to tailor programs to the unique needs and preferences of their citizens.

- They are much more cost conscious because they don't have the luxury of a federal credit card; and they are able to learn from each other.

This last point might be the most critical of all. When we turn to Washington for answers, we get a single one-size-fits-all solution. When we turn to states and local communities, and ultimately to their citizens, we essentially say, "Here is your money back. Go ahead and try new approaches." This is precisely what Supreme Court Justice Louis Brandeis had in mind when he made his famous pronouncement that states should serve as "laboratories of democracy."

This isn't just ivory-towered theory. Every day we see states and communities generally initiating bold and pioneering new approaches to crime control, welfare dependency, education reform, and economic development. Gov. John Engler of Michigan calls the new reformist spirit "the counterrevolution in state government."

States aren't waiting for federal action to get their economies moving. This year more than fifteen governors are expected to sign growth-oriented tax cuts to expand business investment in their states. While Washington has debated a capital-gains tax cut ad nauseam for eight years now (although we passed the measure out of the House in one hundred days as part of our *Contract with America*), Mississippi and Colorado in 1994 abolished their state capital-gains tax *entirely* for new investment inside their respective states. New York is now expected to do the same.

In the area of crime prevention, many states have enacted "three-strikes-and-you're-out" laws requiring life imprisonment for a third felony conviction. In Virginia, Gov. George Allen now requires that at least one crime victim sit on every parole board. Several other states have moved to abolish parole altogether.

Or consider the blizzard of reforms in the education area. Over half the states are now experimenting with open enrollment, magnet schools, and other programs that allow parents to send their kids to a selection of public schools. Massachusetts Gov. William Weld pushed through a bill that virtually abolishes the most indefensible of the education Establishment's longstanding sacred cows: teacher tenure. "Talent and not tenure should determine who is leading our classrooms," says Weld.

Wisconsin has become the national test case in a trial education voucher program that allows state funds to be used to send 550 low-income Milwaukee youth to private schools. The program's torchbearer, Polly Williams, is a black Democratic assemblywoman who served as a Jesse Jackson delegate in 1988. Williams and Gov. Tommy Thompson want to vastly expand the program to more families in what may become the nation's first statewide education voucher program.

Not all of these reforms will work, of course. But one thing is certain: you will never see this kind of experimentation coming from Washington, D.C.

THE TENTH AMENDMENT REVISITED

Perhaps the most important reason to turn back many activities back to the states is that we have a constitutional imperative to do so. Washington policymakers for too long have ignored the Tenth Amendment which states the Founders' intention quite clearly and unambiguously: "The powers not delegated to the United States by the Constitution, nor prohibited by it to the States, are reserved to the States respectively, or to the people."

In other words, the federal government derives its powers from the states, not the other way around. The unfortunate political reality these days is that power flows in exactly the reverse direction than was originally intended. "Our straying from this principle of limited government is among the reasons America seems to have gotten so badly off track," says Senate Majority Leader Bob Dole. One consequence of the dismantling of the Tenth Amendment is that government has become increasingly distant from the citizens who pay for it. Most of the growth of government during this century has been at the federal level, not the state or local level. The figures below highlight the disturbing trend:

Percent of Government Spending by:

	Local Government	Federal Government
1900	60%	20%
1940	23%	52%
1960	21%	65%
1990	19%	67%

This federalization of power has made government at best an irrelevancy to the lives of middle-income working Americans. It explains why so many Americans believe they have lost control over their government.

A NEW PARTNERSHIP

In the past when mayors and governors heard talk in Washington of turning back federal programs to their states and cities they let out a loud groan. Usually this meant a kind of shift-and-shaft federalism, whereby Congress cut the funds but kept handing down to lower levels of government the expensive rules, regulations, and mandates.

Over the past ten years, states and cities have been innocent victims of Congress's regulatory big stick. At a 1993 press conference protesting federal buck-passing, Chicago Mayor Richard M. Daley, a Democrat, complained that "Washington has sent us in the last year alone an eleven-foot stack of new rules and regulations." Mayor Daley said the city of Chicago had the equivalent of two full-time workers signing nearly 150,000 federal forms every year. Frank Shafroth, spokesman for the National League of Cities, has complained that "EPA rules seem to be written in Latin with Greek footnotes."

The cost is huge. Some cities, such as Columbus, Ohio, have calculated that federal rules raise city taxes by about $500 per family. Having proven we can't balance our own budget, Washington lawmakers have been doing everything we can to make sure cities and states can't balance theirs either.

That game in Washington is over. We're ending the travesty of mandates without money. Our *Contract with America* placed new restrictions on the passage of these pass-the-buck regulations. Here is what we enacted:

The Unfunded Mandate Reform Act, which requires federal agencies to minimize the unfunded mandates they impose on communities; requires Congress to prepare cost estimates for any bill that imposes an unfunded mandate on states or cities; and imposes new legislative restrictions on the enactment of bills with unfunded mandates of $50 million or more.

Next, as we begin to return program responsibility back to states and cities through block grants, we pledge to reduce the regulatory strings attached to those dollars. We also want to impose a mandate moratorium—a kind of regulatory "time out"—until we've had a chance to comprehensively review and roll back the mudslide of rules Democratic Congresses have choked our states and cities with over the last ten years. Governors and mayors ask Congress: give us less money, but give us the flexibility to solve our own problems our own ways. This productive new partnership with states and cities will help us balance our budget—and will help them balance theirs.

STEP THREE: TAP THE GENIUS AND GENEROSITY OF OUR CITIZENS

Ultimately, the solution to our social, economic, and moral problems in America will not be solved by state or local governments but rather through the genius and goodness of the American people and our private institutions. This means that we need to directly challenge the fundamental elitism underlying much of modern liberal governance. Liberal elites believe ordinary Americans aren't always capable of making sound decisions for themselves. They feel it's better to let Washington's "best and brightest" make decisions. This is why they have spent nearly a half century erecting a protective "nanny state" on the banks of the Potomac.

This is also why our $500-per-child tax credit is an arrow through the heart of the philosophy of liberalism. Liberals truly don't believe that working families in America—and remember, three-quarters of our tax cut went straight into the wallets of low- and middle-income families—can spend $500 or even $1,000 as wisely as can bureaucrats.

This is the great divide today between liberals and conservatives. To the fullest extent possible, we want to empower ordinary people to make decisions for themselves. Below are several examples of policies we support because they give more decisionmaking power back to American citizens:

• We want to give parents of all incomes the choice wealthy parents have today: which school they want their child to attend.

• We want to expand Individual Retirement Accounts so Americans can rely more on personal savings accounts that they manage themselves and less on government social insurance programs to take care of them when they retire.

- We want to institute a debt buy-down policy which empowers taxpayers to devote up to 10 percent of their income tax dollars for the purpose of reducing the national debt.

- We want term limits so we can have genuine citizen legislators in Washington making policy decisions rather than elite, professional politicians.

- We want to give Americans the option of Medical Savings Accounts, whereby citizens can have vastly expanded control over their own health-care dollars and can become cost-conscious health-care consumers, thus saving money.

- We want to give back to citizens their basic Fifth Amendment property rights and prohibit the government from "taking" private property without just compensation.

It's time to dump the Washington command-and-control model and give citizens more command and control over their own lives.

CREATING A CIVIL SOCIETY

If we return power to the citizens and downsize Washington, then we must also rely more heavily on private initiatives as a replacement for government programs that haven't worked. We must tap into organizations such as the Boys and Girls Clubs, the Salvation Army, churches, and thousands of nonprofit and volunteer efforts to help people in need of support.

Private institutions work better as social problem-solvers. A study by the National Center for Policy Analysis in Dallas found that private agencies out-perform government in providing foster care, job training, alcohol and drug abuse rehab, and many other social service areas. For example, in 1992 the private nonprofit group Committee for Creative Non-Violence (CCNV) spent $365,000 to house 1,400 homeless people. The District of Columbia government, using its own and federal money, spent $26 million to house 1,400 homeless individuals. In other words, the city government spent thirty-five times more to provide shelter for a homeless person than did the private group.

When the Salvation Army takes care of the homeless, the organization requires the recipients of the aid to get up in the morning, make their bed, wash their dishes, earn their keep, and look for a job. It tries to build up the homeless person's self-esteem and sense of personal responsibility. Behavioral improvement is a condition of continued aid. By contrast, with government programs the assistance is an entitlement— nothing is asked in return for the help. Not surprisingly, when the homeless are in the Salvation Army shelters they get back on their feet and return to work much more frequently than do those in government housing programs.

Often well-intentioned government programs only reward the kind of irresponsible behavior that we would never tolerate in our own homes. Father Jerry

Hill, who runs a private homeless shelter in Dallas, complains that some government programs actually hinder private efforts to help people get back on their feet. Social Security disability programs pay as much as $446 a month to addicts. "I can't help them," Father Hill says, "when they have that kind of money to support their habit."

The American people are caring, compassionate, and charitable. We are a nation of good neighbors. Six out of ten Americans do unpaid volunteer work during the year—a higher percentage than any other industrial nation. In the 1980s, the supposed "decade of greed," we saw an explosion of private charitable giving, reaching $120 billion in 1992. When the value of volunteered time is added to the dollar giving, private charity is about as large as public welfare.

The liberal mindset thinks that if we don't do it in Washington, the job won't get done. We believe that all too often when Washington feels compelled to intervene always and everywhere, too often the private sector retreats and the job never gets done.

This, in fact, was a central theme of Pope John Paul II's 1991 encyclical letter. In discussing the rise of what he calls the "Social Assistance State"—which we in America refer to as the "welfare state"—he laments the usurpation of the traditional roles of charities, communities, and family. His message bears repeating because it runs parallel to what we are trying to accomplish: "By intervening directly and depriving society of its responsibility, the Social Assistance State leads to a loss of human energies and an inordinate increase of public agencies, which are dominated more by bureaucratic ways of thinking than by concern for serving their clients, and which are accompanied by an enormous increase in spending. In fact, it would appear that needs are best understood and satisfied by people who are closest to them and act as neighbors to those in need. It should be added that certain kinds of demands often call for a response which is not simply material but which is capable of perceiving the deeper human need."

Then Pope John Paul II emphasized that the downtrodden cannot improve their condition with only financial and material support. "One thinks of the condition of refugees, immigrants, the elderly, the sick, and all those in circumstances which call for assistance, such as drug abusers: all these people can be helped effectively only by those who offer them genuine fraternal support, in addition to the necessary care."

Government, even when working at its best, is incapable of providing this kind of essential fraternal support. And indeed studies show that when low-income people are truly in crisis, they turn first to friends and neighbors for support, not government. When we say that we need to rely more on the genius and goodness of all our citizens to foster genuine solutions to our social, economic, and moral problems, we are calling for a return to what once was called a "civil society." This is the Jeffersonian notion—long accepted in this nation until the birth of the modern welfare state—that America needed effective but limited government in order to liberate people to engage in civic responsibility. Civic responsibility meant being a good citizen. With amazing clarity of vision, Jefferson predicted that the larger government grew, the more it would crowd out individual responsibility in a civil society.

Ultimately this means that we as Americans have a challenge ahead: if we really want less government, a balanced budget, and more freedom, then all of us as citizens have to take greater responsibility in our homes and in our neighborhoods. Civility and the basic duties of good citizenship need to start serving as replacements for government spending.

If we succeed in our mission to balance the budget, topple failed bureaucracies, and send power back home, then we are convinced more Americans will start taking citizenship seriously again. When we start looking to local residents to solve local problems, we will discover creative, flexible, and cost-effective remedies to the very social problems that for government policymakers have for so long seemed hopelessly insoluble.

10

The Courage to Change

AMERICA HAS ARRIVED at an historic moment. Having won the Cold War and vanquished the communist menace, can this powerful and prosperous nation come together and make a national commitment to balance the federal budget? Can we end the system of passing the buck to our children and grandchildren and start paying our own bills? Can we regain control of our economic destiny?

Every American knows that we must do so soon—even the most liberal of Democrats know it in their hearts. A great nation does not run massive budget deficits during peacetime. If America is to fulfill its role as the leader of the Free World in the next century (and if not us, who?), we must first solve our economic problems at home. Just as communism was a dark and formidable evil that imperiled our national security and the future of freedom, so it is that our burgeoning national debt now imperils America's economic security and the future of our free institutions.

We have freely admitted throughout this book that we don't have all the answers to balancing the budget. But what we do have is something that has been lacking for twenty-five years in Congress: an ironclad resolve to eliminate the deficit by 2002 and then keep it balanced.

We will surely make mistakes. No one will agree with all our spending priorities. We'll certainly infuriate Washington's liberal Establishment, which seems quite content to preserve the status quo and proclaim, "Don't worry, be happy!" They are much like the man who, while falling off a twenty-story building, says, as he drops past the fifth floor, "So far, so good."

Special-interest groups and the media will no doubt demonize us for taking away Washington's credit card. They will rant and rave that our budget is too tough and that it causes too much pain and sacrifice. And to some extent they will be right. Our budget will cause sacrifice. But mostly we are requiring Washington to sacrifice, not American families.

We also reject the prevalent attitude in Washington that the best way to attack the deficit is to tax families first. If a choice must be made between shrinking the federal budget and shrinking the family budget, Washington liberals will start reaching for the taxpayers' wallets. They won't succeed on our watch.

We are sincere in our efforts to try to forge a bipartisan plan with our colleagues in the Democratic party and with President Clinton to solve the crisis of deficit spending. This is no time for partisan squabbling. We are open to any and all good-faith Democratic proposals—except those that involve new taxes, of course—and are hopeful that just as many of our *Contract with America* items garnered more than 50 percent support from the Democrats, many of these same members will join our journey to reach a balanced budget. The stakes are high; but so is the payoff. We have said repeatedly to the President and the Democratic leadership in Congress: if you don't like features of our budget-balancing plan, we are eager to see how you would propose to do it. So far, no serious White House proposal to balance the budget has been forthcoming. If the President simply refuses to lead on this issue, it is our profoundest hope that he will at least follow rather than obstruct.

But the truth is, in the end it doesn't matter to us if the special-interest groups oppose us, if liberal Democrats oppose us, or even if the President opposes us. What matters, ultimately, is that we have the support of the American people. If the American public agrees with us that this vital challenge of balancing the federal budget must be met—then it will be.

A SHARED COMMITMENT

What can you as a citizen do to help balance the budget and improve our government? First, it's important to remember that this nation's greatness rests on the combined impact of small acts of greatness by millions of ordinary citizens. During his first presidential inauguration in 1981, Ronald Reagan recounted this inspiring story of a single American hero who did his small but important part to help the cause of freedom: "Martin Treptow left his job in a small town barber shop in 1917 to go to France with the famed Rainbow Division. There, on the Western Front, he was killed trying to carry a message between battalions under heavy artillery fire. We are told that on his body was found a diary. On the flyleaf, under the heading, "My Pledge," he had written these words: 'America must win this war. Therefore, I will work, I will save, I will sacrifice, I will endure, I will fight cheerfully and do my utmost, as if the issue of the whole struggle depended on me alone.' "

Of course the struggle that we face today requires nowhere near the work and sacrifice that was required of Martin Treptow or the many millions of Americans who have worn the American military uniform, fought and, in some cases, died for the cause of our freedoms. Mostly what is required of every member of this generation is the courage and commitment to begin to change our government for the good of future generations.

We pledged at the outset of this book that our efforts to balance the budget would be made in cooperation and consultation with the American people. Quite frankly, we need your help. On page 233 you will find what we call the "Balanced Budget Questionnaire." This questionnaire asks your advice on many of the ideas presented in this book. We need to rely on the collective wisdom of the American public to solve a crisis of this dimension. (We've emphasized throughout this book that it's futile to search for the solutions to our problems in Washington. Solutions to problems like these, which were *caused* in Washington, can't be solved there.) So please, take the time to fill out your Balanced Budget Questionnaire and send it to Speaker Newt Gingrich.

A VISION OF AMERICA

It is the year 2003. It is Monday morning. No American was murdered over the weekend. Every child in America is attending a first-rate school in which he or she is learning in an environment of safety, not violence. Where there was once the desolation of public housing, there is now the pride of home ownership and urban renewal. Teenagers are not having babies out of wedlock or doing drugs; they are in high school or college preparing to compete and win in the information age. America now lives under a tax code that rewards work, risk taking, saving for the future, and entrepreneurship. Businesses are moving into rather than out of our cities, which once again are becoming symbols of America's economic might. In short: America is back at work.

And as Americans get in their cars to go to school or work, they turn on the radio and celebrate the morning news flash report: for the first time in more than thirty years, the U.S. government ran a budget surplus last year. This is the future that we envision for America. It is called the American Dream.

THE BALANCED BUDGET
QUESTIONNAIRE

Your voice counts. Tell us what you think about various approaches to balancing the budget. Please answer the following questions and send this page to Speaker of the House Newt Gingrich, 233 U.S. Capitol Building, Washington, D.C. 20515.

	AGREE	DISAGREE
• *Balancing the federal budget should be the top priority of this Congress.*	❑	❑
• *Taxes should be raised to balance the budget.*	❑	❑
• *Defense spending has already been cut too much.*	❑	❑
• *Congress should cut its own budget and staff.*	❑	❑
• *We can reduce the deficit by eliminating waste, pork, and bureaucracy.*	❑	❑
• *Foreign aid should be substantially reduced.*	❑	❑

	AGREE	DISAGREE
• *We should take big business off the dole by cutting corporate welfare.*	❑	❑
• *Taxpayer assistance for the Corporation for Public Broadcasting should end.*	❑	❑
• *We should start to privatize Amtrak.*	❑	❑
• *We should privatize public housing.*	❑	❑
• *Congress spends money on programs that exceed its constitutional authority.*	❑	❑
• *More federal activities should be turned over to states and communities.*	❑	❑

• *What other programs should be reformed, reorganized, reduced or eliminated?*

_____

_____

_____

ABOUT THE EDITOR

STEPHEN MOORE is director of fiscal policy at the Cato Institute in Washington, D.C. A former senior economist at the Joint Economic Committee for Rep. Dick Armey of Texas, Moore is a regular contributor to numerous publications, including *The Wall Street Journal*, *Human Events*, the *National Review*, *The New York Times*, and *Readers Digest*. A native of Chicago, Moore is a graduate of the University of Illinois. He completed his graduate studies in economics at George Mason University. He lives with his wife, Allison, and his sons, Justin and William, in Arlington, Virginia.